BIGGER FISH TO FRY

New Anthropologies of Europe: Perspectives and Provocations

Series Editors:
Michael Herzfeld, *Harvard University*; **Melissa L. Caldwell,** *UC Santa Cruz*

The anthropology of Europe has dramatically shifted ground from its emergence in descriptive ethnography to the exploration of innovative theoretical and methodological approaches today. This well-established series, relaunched by Berghahn Books with a new subtitle, invites proposals that speak to contemporary social and cultural theory through innovative ethnography and vivid description. Topics range from migration, human rights, and humanitarianism to historical, visual, and material anthropology to the neoliberal and audit-culture politics of Schengen and the European Union.

Volume 3
Bigger Fish to Fry: A Theory of Cooking as Risk, with Greek Examples
David E. Sutton

Volume 2
Vertiginous Life: An Anthropology of Time and the Unforeseen
Daniel M. Knight

Volume 1
Modernity and the Unmaking of Men
Violeta Schubert

BIGGER FISH TO FRY

A Theory of Cooking as Risk, with Greek Examples

David E. Sutton

berghahn
NEW YORK · OXFORD
www.berghahnbooks.com

First published in 2021 by

Berghahn Books

www.berghahnbooks.com

© 2021, 2023 David E. Sutton
First paperback edition published in 2023

Library of Congress Cataloging-in-Publication Data

A C.I.P. cataloging record is available from the Library of Congress
Library of Congress Cataloging in Publication Control Number: 2021032926

British Library Cataloguing in Publication Data

A catalogue record for this book is available from the British Library

ISBN 978-1-80073-223-0 hardback
ISBN 978-1-80539-113-5 paperback
ISBN 978-1-80539-370-2 epub
ISBN 978-1-80073-224-7 web pdf

https://doi.org/10.3167/9781800732230

To my wife Bethany Rowe, my cooking companion (sharer of bread)
for forty years of kitchen surprises and successes, mundane and spectacular

CONTENTS

⚜

FIGURES

❧

PREFACE

❧

One of the jokes I remember my father telling when I was a child was about blintzes. In it, a poor Jewish man named Moishe observes a presumably much wealthier man through the window of a restaurant, absorbed in enjoying a plate of cheese blintzes. He returns home to his wife, Becky, and asks her to make him some blintzes so he too can enjoy this wonderful dish. She replies "You want me to make blintzes, Moishe? But we don't have cheese." "So, make it without cheese," he replies. "But, Moishe, we don't have butter either." Undeterred, he encourages her, "So make it without butter." She shrugs and goes into the kitchen only to return twenty minutes later with a plate full of blintzes. The man gazes at them eagerly, takes a bite, chews for a bit, and then turns to his wife and says, "You know, Becky, I don't know what these rich people see in blintzes."

I liked this joke and could get the point even around the age of eight: blintzes were not the same when you removed key ingredients. I had more difficulty with another joke involving the dumpling dish kreplach. The mother of a boy who for some strange reason had developed an overwhelming fear of kreplach slowly deconstructs the dish, showing him each ingredient and how it is added to the dish. I can almost see my father's half smile and gestures as he tells it "Look, son, it's only a meatball; look, son, it's only a pancake, while the boy echoes 'only a meatball, only a pancake.'" The boy is fine until the very end when she puts the final touches on the dish by dropping the dumpling into the soup, at which point the boy screams, "Ahh! Kreplach!"

At the time I found this joke challenging—I couldn't make the connection between the joke and the idea of the whole being greater than the sum of the parts, even after my father had explained it. I can now recognize a certain similarity to the first joke (of course, any joke that requires explaining is doomed). But both of them stuck with me as part of my childhood experience of thinking about the relationship between dishes and their ingredients as I started to learn the elements of cooking from my father and other adults in our circle. Take away one key ingredient and you spoil the dish, as many grandmothers, hiding their recipes from the inquisitive, seem to know. But on the other hand, add too much of something else, and perhaps you lose the meaning of the dish as well. One of my mother's graduate students (and subsequent lifelong colleague and friend) Sue Barrow, for example, taught me at age five or six that you couldn't make up for too much salt in a cookie dough batter by adding more sugar (I was so fascinated by the notion that cookies contained salt that a pinch was not at all satisfying to me). At the same time, I feel that I was on the cusp of understanding something else: mistakes might possibly be fixed, mid-stream, if one knows enough, a theme explored in chapter 3. Certainly, my early recipe making was my first experience with parts that created greater wholes, and how the whole might be destroyed by a missing part, a good foundation for the holistic thinking that eventually drew me to my mother's passion: anthropology.

Many years and a lifetime of meals gone by, I find myself firmly ensconced in researching food from an anthropological perspective. But while I've tried over the course of the past twenty or more years to explore a variety of theoretical topics—materiality, memory, the senses, situated knowledge—through the medium of food; the mundane everyday aspects of putting together a recipe and having it come out "the same" or "different" seem to suggest unanswered theoretical questions that still tickle my brain, and my palate, and that I explore in these pages.

Meanwhile, my non-food related research had focused on questions of historical consciousness, temporality, or to put it in old-fashioned terms, continuity and change. I had been wanting to think about these issues in relationship to food, but not by writing a history of the origins of particular foodstuffs or even particular styles from a mile away. Rather, I wanted to combine the ethnographic sensibilities I had been developing on the island of Kalymnos since I began fieldwork there in the early 1990s, with a sense of how it might be possible to think about changing foods and dishes at the micro-level. While I had some inkling at least since the early 2000s that Marshall Sahlins's work combining anthropology and history might have something to do with this, when I started working in earnest on studying everyday cooking, I found that some ideas take longer than others to germinate or "bake" as they say in Greece. So I was always thinking about this question while working on *Secrets from the Greek Kitchen*, my ethnography of cooking on Kalymnos. But that project took me, for the most part, in different directions, given that my methodology for that project focused on video recordings, which led me into questions about the kitchen as environment, gender relations and power, and the agency of kitchen objects. While I had developed my thoughts on food and memory in *Remembrance of Repasts*, I felt that book led me in a direction perhaps too focused on the past, rather than on temporality and the relation of past, present, and future, as I try to do in this book. In some ways, then, this book has turned into a manifesto for how someone could do a future ethnography of cooking that focuses not on the present kitchen environment, social relationships, and styles of cooking, nor on memories of the past instantiated and embodied through cooking. Rather, the ethnography I have in mind would include all of those through the lens of a long-term ethnographic project that would track people as they make "the same" dishes over and over, yet at least a little bit differently each time. It is here that I hope to show that cooking can stand in for all kinds of cultural processes that we wish to understand in their constant mutability and constancy. And here I thank my mother, Constance "Connie" Sutton, who died before I completed this manuscript. And while she was perhaps puzzled that I could still be writing about food, she encouraged me always to be thinking about continuity and change or "changing continuities" as she called them.

As I chose the title *Bigger Fish to Fry* to stand for the ways that small cooking changes can have larger significance, I'm put in mind of one particular big fish that I wrote about with my colleague Peter Wogan: *Jaws* (2009). *Jaws* was on a lot of people's minds in the summer of 2020, not just because of another milestone, the forty-fifth anniversary of its opening. It was more because a lot of people were wondering which of our many politicians (mostly Republican governors) was most like the mayor of Amity, demanding that the beaches had to be reopened for business, no matter the risk. But for me it was in looking for a "bigger boat" to catch the big fish of a theory of cooking that *Jaws* was still resonating. And while humans eat more sharks than the other way around, *Jaws* also raises the issue of risk in a very palpable way, an issue motivating my approach in this book. So, for that matter, does the book's cover picture, James Ensor's 1896 painting *The Dangerous Cooks*. Ensor's restaurant setting is not particularly restorative, and it is a male-dominated space different from the kitchen spaces of the (mostly) women on the island of Kalymnos, Greece, from which I draw insights. Ensor seems to use cooking in a more metaphorical sense—critics as cannibals, the artist as sacrificial victim. But his painting also suggests to me the danger, or risk, of categories in flux—eater and eaten, human and animal—as well as some recipes that might be overdue for modification. Some of the categories at risk in these pages are no doubt more mundane, but no less significant for that. *Bon Appétit!*

ACKNOWLEDGMENTS

I've probably chewed these ideas over with so many colleagues over the years that they are bored hearing more jawboning about it, but I'm grateful for those who had the patience to listen and to read some of the pieces of this project along the way. But none more patient in this case than Leonidas Vournelis, who has heard these ideas hatched many times and patiently helped me parse through some of the details both theoretical and ethnographic. Leo's voice is always in my head. Three other colleagues who patiently talked through some of these with me from the vantage point of their own understanding of Greek food and cooking are Neni Panourgia, Nafsika Papacharalampous, and Stavroula Pipyrou, and I'm grateful for their time and friendship and contributions in this text, noted and not. I talked this over with some colleagues both in my own head, that is, in dialogue with their work, as well as in real-time, non-socially distanced conversations over the years. I would especially like to thank, in no particular order, Yiannis Hamilakis, Daniel Knight, Olga Kalentzidou, Dimitris Theodossopoulos (along with memorable *spanakorizo*), Charles Stewart, Renee Hirschon, Nick Argenti, Vassiliki Yiakoumaki, Krishnendu Ray, and Amy Trubek. Special thanks in this regard to Richard Wilk, who generously and regularly invited me to his home for much delicious food and conversation. Eleana Yalouri has shared her kitchen passions with me, our convergent interests in material culture and the senses, as well as some wonderful Greek-Thai meals that we cooked together in her home during my many visits there. Peter Wogan has been my constant collaborator and intellectual companion through this and other trips, always ready to make room in his bigger boat (or bigger hot tub) to anchor my musings with tough but stimulating questions. Jim and Renate Fernandez have nourished me in too many ways to acknowledge, as we exchanged thoughts about tasty tropes about stinky cheese and satisfying soup over the years. Antonio Lauria has cooked some amazing pasta and provided stimulating conversation in difficult times.

On Kalymnos, I'm grateful to all those who have been such generous friends and hosts since I began fieldwork on Kalymnos and even before. But particularly Aggeliki Roditi, whose home became a home away from home for me during the course of this research, and who introduced me to a favorite Kalymnian snack of egg with tomato (*avgozoumi*). Also, her son Dimitris and his wife Evdokia Passa, the latter whose cooking is second to none on Kalymnos. Katina Miha and her husband Nikolas and daughter Katerina have been my most generous friends over the forty years I have been visiting Kalymnos, and my debt to them, and to Katina's mother Katerina who passed in 2012, is reflected in every page of this book. Katina passed away in late 2020 as I was just finishing this book. She always called me "brother" and I called her "sister." I learned so much from her over the years about Kalymnian cooking and its embeddedness in social life, and I owe many insights in this book to her. I miss her already. I also have a tremendous debt to Nina Papamihail and her husband Manolis. Nina's patience in reconstructing weeks and weeks of meals over the past ten or more years has been truly astonishing, and helpful in my thinking about repetition and change. And a sincere thanks to Polykseni Miha and the many other Kalymnians who have become used to my presence and curiosity in their lives.

A precis of this argument, mostly reflected in chapter 1, was published as an article in *Anthropological Theory* in 2018 under the title "Cooking in Theory: Risky Events in the Structure of the Conjuncture." I am particularly grateful to Steve Reyna and Nina Glick-Schiller, lifetime friends, for their guidance in that process, and for their always probing questions. Thanks also to Jakob Klein and Harry West for inviting me to present an earlier version of this article at the SOAS food forum Nkumi writing group in 2016, and for the feedback I received there. I was able to further refine some of the key ideas during a fellowship in 2018 in Durham, UK. I am grateful to the Durham University Institute for Advanced Studies and to St. Cuthbert's Society and Elizabeth Archibald, whose hosting I won't soon forget. And to Durham Anthropology Department and Elisabeth Kirtsoglou, my "buddy" and most thoughtful colleague. At the Institute, special thanks to Linda Crowe, Sam Hillyard, and Nick "better call" Saul, and my fellow fellow Tammy Kohn for making my stay so enjoyable and stimulating.

I appreciate the support of the series editors, Michael Herzfeld and Lissa Caldwell, in providing guidance and encouragement. As well as all the work by Tom Bonnington and the rest of the crew at Berghahn.

Finally, my sons Sam and Max contributed to this book in important ways. Sam through his careful recovery of video footage from which he generated some of the photo illustrations in the book. And Max through his meticulous editing of several chapters. And both of them for being willing guinea pigs for some of my cooking experiments over many years.

IN THE DANGEROUS KITCHEN

COOKING MATTERS

"What should we have for dinner?" Mary Douglas (1974) asked this question in her classic article on the subject as a way to get at the cultural categories by which we define various kinds of meals. But in her family struggles over whether to have soup and a sandwich, or some combination thereof, she expressed no concern regarding how the ingredients might be assembled, processed, and cooked to create these dishes. I often have similar discussions with my own family (or in my head) about what to make for dinner. The other night, I decided on a Greek salad, which I had made a number of times in the past week to take advantage of the fresh tomatoes and cucumbers from the local farmer's market. Having cut a lovely orange tomato, and halfway through cutting an onion, I remembered that I had half a can of refried beans in the refrigerator that really needed to be used up. I thought, perhaps instead of a Greek salad, I should make soft tacos. All of a sudden, I saw myself putting the chopped tomato into a food processor so I could sauté it with the beans, onion, some mushrooms that might not last much longer, and the leftover brown rice that my son had made earlier that day as part of his "bulking up" diet. Soft tacos it was, but not quite the same soft tacos that I had made before. As I chewed on my tacos, I wondered: was there the kernel of an interesting anthropological idea in these mundane cooking contingencies?

Beyond simple contingencies, I realized that there was a *risk* involved here. Because, in throwing together a dish—say, a stir fry that can contain a number of potential ingredients—one could go too far and add something that simply didn't belong, that didn't taste right, or that didn't go with the other ingredients, as I indeed found out when trying to add leftover salmon to a stir-fry. Or, in moments of indecision about ingredients, I might add them in the wrong order; in my distraction, I might let the broccoli steam, which is a disaster for a decent stir-fry. At risk was not simply the potential for a good or bad meal, but much more: my own sense of myself as a competent cook and the opinions of others (in this case, my family members) as to my level of skill. Much more was at stake in these mundane decisions than a mere intellectual puzzle but rather something concerning "skill." Since time is finite, I wondered as well whether my cooking represented time well-utilized or opportunities wasted. What might an anthropology of cooking reveal about these concerns?

There has been a striking, cross-disciplinary growth in food studies over roughly the past thirty years, representing a broad rethinking of aspects of food production, exchange, consumption, and disposal. Anthropology, which has shown less neglect toward the significance of food than many other disciplines, has also revitalized its interests in aspects of the social, sensory, symbolic, and biological ramifications of food, as well as their intersections. Food has provided an impetus to rethink aspects of classic anthropological topics including kinship, exchange, and material culture, as well as a stimulus to expanding more recent interests in power and resistance, materiality and consumption, memory and identity, and the phenomenology of everyday (sensory) experience. Food has been the subject of multisited ethnographies and has provided new anthropological approaches to history. It is certainly a good time to take seriously Claude Levi-Strauss's claim that food is "Good to Think."

Scholarly interest in cooking, however, has yet to catch up with this new wave, notwithstanding Levi-Strauss's view of its centrality in the so-called transition from "nature to culture." With a few notable exceptions, cooking has been largely neglected as an ethnographic topic in contemporary food studies, and even more so as a site of theoretical reflection. Elsewhere (Sutton 2016a) I have explored some of the reasons for this, as well as some of the notable exceptions. Cooking, has, for example, been thematized in a number of recent studies of gender, identity, knowledge, and power.[1] It has also been given attention by a few scholars interested in material culture studies and the ways that cooking creates certain kinds of culturally mediated transformations of substances and socialities.[2] In my own ethnographic work, I have explored some of the ways that cooking might be used to think about the relationship between skill, embodiment, and everyday life. Here, however, I want to argue for a different potential trajectory for cooking theory by suggesting that an approach to cooking as *everyday risk* can offer new insights into the question "what is cooking?" while also providing a topic for ethnographic research that can push certain theoretical perspectives forward in new ways.

It is clear that cooking has not been taken seriously, both because of what it is—a repetitive, daily task—and who performs it. On the former, historian of cooking Michael Symons points out that the very "repetitiveness of cooking is part of the reason why many Western intellectuals have snubbed it" (Symons 2003: 26). However, the notion of repetitiveness requires a point of view on what is similar and what is different[3] and is one of the things that makes cooking potentially valuable to anthropologists employing an ethnographic approach. On the latter point—who does the cooking—Krishnendu Ray notes that cooking has been treated as trivial in the academy, at the same time music and architecture were taken very seriously: "triviality is linked basically to the inferiority of the subject—it is mostly women and mostly poor people who do most of the cooking in most parts of the world. That's still not taken seriously in the higher reaches of even the cultural academy of men theorizing."[4] Or, cooking may be segmented into that which is "interesting," i.e., done by professional chefs, and the repetitive drudgery of everyday cooking done by women, a theme that runs through much literature on cooking. As Vicki Swinbank notes, however, this is often a matter of perspective, as women downplay their originality and stress the ways they share knowledge within a cooking community, while male professional chefs "draw upon the traditional recipes of these women, without giving due acknowledgement, often elaborating on these recipes in order to claim them as their own" (2002: 470). Furthermore, Swinbank argues that it is the "very everydayness of women's domestic cooking that causes it to be overlooked and not counted as culture. The largely non-individualistic, collective tradition of women's cooking is generally dismissed by male intellectuals, who consider that only the 'exceptional and the extraordinary' constitute culture" (2002: 478).

I have more to say on the "exceptional and the extraordinary" below. But it seems to me that one of the advantages that the study of cooking offers is that it is indeed an everyday practice, which, while perhaps "mundane" to some, is never exactly the same from one day to the next. It is always caught up in the contingencies of social situations, changing environments, recalcitrant ingredients, and ordinary creativity. In her groundbreaking book *Kitchen Secrets: The Meaning of Cooking in Everyday Life*, Frances Short (2006) documents the many "skills" involved in an expansive understanding of cooking that includes the frenetic balancing of daily contingencies, caring and coping with (familial, one's own) preferences, and the demands of life. She suggests a person-centered, rather than task-centered, understanding of cooking, a contrast she describes as follows:

> A task-centred perspective might see making bread as requiring or utilizing a range of techniques, including mixing, kneading, rolling and shaping. A person-centred ap-

proach, on the other hand, would take into consideration the perceptual, conceptual, emotional and logistical cooking skills used or required by the cook and the circumstances or context in which making the bread took place. (2006: 61)

While in my own work I found it worthwhile to blur the line between "persons" and "tasks" (Sutton 2014: chap. 2), Short's work was an inspiration in showing how much ethnographically interesting stuff might go into preparing a meal that was not in any other sense special or unusual.

At the same time, it is necessary to note that, as food scholars have been showing for the past twenty years, food is not irrelevant to wider sociopolitical concerns; its mundaneness is also part of its ability to entwine issues of gender, class, race, and identities on multiple scales in the pragmatics of daily life. As Wim Van Daele notes, food almost seems unavoidable as a topic for anthropologists, given their interest in how people live their lives. Those who did write about it, in studies of small-scale societies,

wrote about food in its connections and entanglements with other aspects of human life and organisation, including political life . . . the wider economy of exchanges . . . and transformations of values in exchanges. As such, food was studied not just in and for itself, as a mere topic, but it also served almost methodologically as a means to study things other than food by way of which food became approached more holistically.[5]

Thus, food is a nexus of activity that can lead to many other issues and understandings of both the structure and everyday negotiation of social processes and cultural meanings. But what might it mean to study "food as food," rather than simply as a window onto something else? This question, posed by Jon Holtzman (2009: 50), reminds us that for all of the value of our holism, we have no trouble reading analyses that take topics such as kinship, exchange, ritual, gender, or migration as central rather than mere windows onto other subjects. And, while the approach to cooking that I am arguing for has much to tell us about many other topics, I would like to start from the idea that studying cooking as cooking is valuable in itself (and not just for the gastronomes among us).

I am thus arguing for the value of thinking about cooking as a kind of everyday risk. This is not meant as a criticism of the extant theoretical approaches to cooking.[6] There is no doubt great value in exploring cooking in terms of gender empowerment and gender oppression, as has become apparent through exciting recent works, as well as thinking of cooking as an art form, a chore, an occupation, or a rich metaphor for cultural processes.[7] I propose *cooking as risk* because it allows me to tie together a number of theoretical approaches that have not previously been applied to cooking. Risk offers something new, a different way to think of cooking as a topic of research, and one that happens to fit rather well with my ethnographic experience of studying cooking on the island of Kalymnos, Greece. The extent to which this is a useful way of thinking about cooking is not limited to my foremost example: Kalymnos. Rather, there might be other places like Kalymnos where everyday risk is, or is not, a trenchant starting point for analyzing cooking.

I employ the word "risk" because it is a useful term in the anthropology of Greece, where my ethnographic work is based, for capturing the confrontation with uncertainty that a number of anthropologists have explored. In addition, risk allows me to engage with several theoretical interventions in the following chapters. First, I address Marshall Sahlins's anthropological approach to history in his famed work on Hawaii, in which he argued for a view of historical process as "the risk of categories in practice" (Sahlins 1985). Cooking is a testing ground for Sahlins's approach and illustrates its strengths as well as potential areas in which it is incomplete. This approach provides a template for the possibility of understanding continuity and change through micro-level research that is attuned, in classic anthropological fashion, to the larger ramifications of the details of everyday life. We have had over thirty years of anthropology that explicitly thematizes change (e.g. Comaroff and Comaroff 1993) while other important voices have argued that we have moved to questions of change while never having truly understood the processes that create continuity (e.g. Connerton 1989).[8] A renewed anthropology of "the event" suggests a focus on what is surprising or unexpected as the key to understanding, even though, as Thijs Van Dooremalen (2017) points out, as a fieldwork strategy it is very hard to plan to study the unexpected. I argue that employing the tools offered by Sahlins's approach allows us to operationalize research that puts itself in the moments when continuity and change happen, and thus to get at Symons's perhaps grandiose comment: "But while each of the cook's actions might be infinitesimal, the results have multiplied into civilisation" (2003: x).

Second, we must consider craft theorist David Pye's notion of the "workmanship of risk" (1968) as a key aspect of craft practice. Pye's concept has been useful in some anthropological approaches to craft (Ingold 2013) and to artisanal food production (Paxson 2013). It contrasts with the "workmanship of certainty" and undermines concerns over the loss of the human aspects of craft practice, one of which Richard Sennett (2008) metonymizes as "the hand" (resonating with Greek linguistic practice of focusing on "the hand" that makes and "the eye" that evaluates in cooking). In focusing on the workmanship of risk, I complement some of the cognitive biases of Sahlins's ideas about "the risk of categories" with an embodied approach. This approach draws on the insights of Ingold and other anthropologists who want to bring our research back to questions of how we learn to do specific tasks in a manner considered skillful. I drew heavily from this method in my ethnography of everyday cooking on Kalymnos (2014). It provided a way to understand the significance of culturally embedded ways of cutting vegetables or rolling out phyllo dough, and what these activities could reveal about the often emergent properties of cooking. In addition, it helps to reveal the problematic directions taken by certain approaches to technology in the kitchen under neoliberal capitalism.

A full understanding of cooking demands that we wed these different approaches that recognize that recipes and other "plans" do play a significant role in cooking, even if they do not in any sense determine the final outcome of the dish. Perhaps there is more in common in the seemingly opposing approaches of a theorist like Sahlins and a theorist like Ingold than meets the eye.

My third substantive chapter engages what Sahlins calls *subjective risk*. This term describes the ways Greek understandings of historical processes—their "historicity" (Stewart 2016)—shape their willingness to embrace and reward risk-taking as an everyday attitude. In studying Kalymnian cooking, one might expect to encounter a discourse about the value of tradition and adherence to the past. In fact, I find a broad cultural acceptance of the notion that value is created through embracing the contingent and risky. While previous anthropological work has ascribed embrace of risk as broadly typical of Greek men, many have ignored the extent to which we find similar values among women, even though they might not explicitly articulate them. Rather, women enact these values in their struggles to establish their identities in a recalcitrant world.

This concept of risk also reveals how Greeks see the relationship between past and future. Notions of time have become more prevalent in anthropological writings on Greece. Yet, these works have not synthesized Greek experiences of time with notions of risk and agency. While I've long been interested in issues that point to the past, the meaning of tradition, and the role of memory in everyday life in Greece (1998, 2001), looking at risk is one way of ensuring that our analysis captures the dynamic tension that always exists between past, present, and future—regardless of whether the people we study are labeled or self-label as "traditional" or "modern." As Jens Zinn (2019: 23–24), paraphrasing John Maynard Keynes, notes: in understanding risk and risk-taking, "Knowledge of the past is valuable but at the same time comes with systematic limits when we are dealing with innovation and the unknowns of the future. This is the case not only for entrepreneurs in the realm of economics but a typical characteristic of everyday life." It is the unfinished nature of cooking and the fact that variation always creeps in (intentionally or unintentionally) that makes it ideal for thinking about this nexus of past-present-future and even for realigning memory with a kind of sensory perception.[9]

Figure 0.1. Alexandra Passa cutting bread in her Kalymnian kitchen. Photo courtesy of Dimitris Roditis.

In conclusion, Greece and Kalymnos are not entirely unique in the broader cultural scene. My theory of cooking as everyday risk is applicable to other kitchens in other times and places. It provides a framework through which we can access cooking across cultures, though no doubt with many cultural particularities in the understanding and enactment of everyday cooking in practice.

DANGEROUS KITCHENS

Frank Zappa, no doubt with tongue in cheek, imagines the kitchen as a dangerous place in his song "The Dangerous Kitchen."[10] It contains lurking hazards of varying degrees of harm—including sharp edges of cans, which we will be considering in chapter 3—making it, indeed, a risk even to enter. It is indisputable that the kitchen presents many physical hazards, especially for the careless cook. As I illustrate when I give formal presentations on Kalymnian cooking, Kalymnian cutting puts one's body, quite literally, at the knife's edge. A cook cradles a long loaf of daily bread against their chest and wields a knife like the bow of a violin. In this pose, the chest constitutes the only oppositional support for the loaf, while the Kalymnian cook creates slice marks in order to more easily tear off portion-sized pieces. But other kinds of risk—such as the cognitive, existential, and interactional types— also lurk in the kitchen.

Allow me to clarify why I use the term "everyday risk," and why the concept of risk is useful, given that it is a term with a long history in the social sciences. One issue with the term "risk" is that it is generally used in a negative sense to refer to undesired outcomes. "The word has been pre-empted to mean bad risks" (Douglas 1992: 24). Social scientists often associate risk with various techniques of risk "management" or "minimization."[11] Limiting risk is the entire point of fields such as safety science and risk analysis, which treat risk as a noun or an objective feature of certain environments. Here, risk is understood in relation to calculation, and the idea is that everything is, in the end, calculable (Zinn 2019: 19). Ulrich Beck famously dubbed modernity "risk society" (1992) because risk is displaced from the local community onto a wider collective that faces various social and ecological catastrophes. Risk is also foisted on the individual who, "increasingly bereft of collective identity and belonging," confronts what Beck calls "biographical risk."[12] This approach is also associated with Anthony Giddens' division of societies into "modern" societies that have lost the stabilizing aspects of the traditional and thus are vulnerable to the anxieties of an unknown future (1999). Such an analysis counterposes the modern with a "traditional" society of stereotypical reproduction of a future much like the past and belief in "fate" as the cause of misfortune (Giddens 1999). Giddens' approach has been roundly criticized in anthropology, and this description of tradition certainly does not apply to the Greece that I knew in the early 1990s.[13] Just as Sahlins' analysis makes continuity and change inseparable aspects of all practice, Greek and Kalymnian cooks find ways to embrace the possibilities afforded by contingency and change as much as they look for continuities in their daily practice, as I will explore in chapter 3. I draw little, then, from this literature on risk society except the idea that there are certain aspects of risk that we can call "objective," though not perhaps in the way meant by Beck and others. As Sahlins argues, and I will explore in the next chapter: every act of reference is a risk, whether intended or not. If I briefly embrace this "objective" understanding, I also would insist, as Zinn argues, that treating risk as a "thing" rather than an "activity" ignores the contextual aspects that are key to understanding risk: "When approaching risk as a process of *doing,* the social aspects more easily enter the debate, since risk does not exist independently of the people, organizations or other social instances, which *perform risk*" (Zinn 2019: 30, emphasis in original).

Alternatively, a long sociological tradition debates the role of risk in relation to capitalist profit, entrepreneurship, and its recent postmodern forms such as "edgework," that is, activities that are engaged in specifically because of the desire to embrace the thrill of risk.[14] As with the social sciences, these subject areas appear distant from this book's concerns. However, such approaches reveal that there is not only objective risk, but also "voluntary risk" in which one willingly exposes oneself to risk for certain purposes (Zinn 2019: 75–77). This fits with the idea that risk is about "interrupting the ordinariness and repetitiveness of life which rewards us with an intensified feeling of being alive" (Zinn 2019: 2).

But what constitutes repetitiveness, and what constitutes an interruption? Feminist critiques of edgework, such as Staci Newmahr's (2011: 686) study of BDSM practices, point out that "the very conceptualization of the edge is gendered." Much theorizing of edgework focuses on physical challenges that stress individualism and self-reliance and usually involve "a romantic, dichotomous tension between the wilderness and civilization" (2011: 689). Newmahr suggests expanding edgework not simply to include women, but also practices that are collaborative and based on emotional work, such as activities that involve trust and pain. This got me thinking more about Kalymnian women's own experiences and definitions of risk. However, Newmahr insists that edgework is defined by extreme experiences, such as sexual experimentation, and that it is a part of the domain of leisure rather than an obligatory or mundane activity.

As I was in the final stages of writing this, my wife drew my attention to an issue of the home and lifestyle magazine *Magnolia Journal* (Issue 15, Summer 2020) titled "A Look at Risk: Choosing Courage to Face the Unknown." This journal is part of the media empire of Joanna and Chip Gaines, most known for their TV series *Fixer Upper* about home renovation. "The Unknown" was no doubt on the minds of many readers of this issue, published as it was in the midst of the COVID-19 lockdown. But the issue only makes very oblique reference to this, noting that "for many of us, reality has shifted. In light of what we've learned and experienced together, there's a chance we understand risk differently than we did before." The issue goes on to discuss all kinds of design and lifestyle elements—food, wallpaper, summer planning, starting a business—as choices we can either approach through caution and certainty or take the risky route. "Once we acknowledge that risk is in every choice we make . . . opportunity appears all around us too" is written on a page with drawings suggesting readers should check the box next to more risky choices, for example, painting your home a new color rather than leaving it the same and never knowing whether you would like it. Throughout the issue, the reader is urged to embrace risk over possible embarrassment, to face choices with courage rather than fear. Mundane risk for sure. But a risk that takes place in a world of individuals (and occasionally families) who only interact with others when they choose to take the risk of opening their homes to others and taking the "risk of being real." It would be easy enough to see this as a particular kind of vision of the neoliberal entrepreneur already, but the issue also includes a feature on Sara Blakely, founder and CEO of Spanx Inc., who writes about being encouraged as a child to fail as often as possible so that she was inured to the embarrassment of risk-taking as an essential part of becoming an entrepreneur. While this mundane example suggests the ubiquity of the "subjective risk" that I will explore in chapter 3, it partakes of a very different vision of risk than that of the "tricks and patents" that I argue is central to Greek kitchen risk-taking.

How might we think of mundane risk not as a free-floating choice made by neoliberal individuals, but rather as embedded in a community life? One evening, over dinner, I was challenged by my long-time friends and colleagues Nina Glick-Schiller and Steve Reyna over whether cooking is, in fact, risky at all. To persuade them, I asked them to imagine a setting in which taste matters deeply on a daily basis. Each meal undergoes an autopsy of its successes and failures and the ability to produce good-tasting food is part of one's reputation. This reputation, while never defined by one particular meal, is built up slowly over a lifetime and is recognized in the community both through daily discussions and the fact that Kalymnian women routinely offer food to neighbors and friends in memory of departed loved ones. Thus, cooking is risky not in the extreme sense of "danger" described above as "edgework," but also because any attempt to simply reproduce or improve a dish—for instance, to try something new or something "traditional" but long forgotten—will be evaluated by a wide group of eaters in a community that places high value on so-called gossip or publicly-circulated reputation.[15] On Kalymnos I found a community that also was very much committed to a shared sense of taste, negotiated and shifting over time, but always part of a wider discourse the community participated in, what Mintz defines as "cuisine," and what I call "gustemology."[16] One such example of embedded risk was provided to me by anthropologist Stavroula Pipyrou, who in making observations about her home village of Kalloni in Northern Greece, notes that women speak of the "danger" involved in trying to cross a "threshold" and take one's cooking to the next level. As she describes:

> Maria (47) was making phyllo for a pie (*pitta*) in the presence of her mother Spiry-doula (77). For those who have experienced the *pitta* of our grandmothers, it is a level of accomplishing something. The *pitta* of our grandmothers is *art,* not nostalgia. It is an objective affirmation of how you make a *pitta*: The color, how you bake it, it is a whole process for just a single *pitta*. The mother Spirydoula was frustrated because Maria wasn't accomplished enough to roll out the phyllo with the rolling pin. And Maria was conscious of the risky situation she had put herself in. That was her own

assessment in which she said "kindinevo" (I am in danger). She was in danger at many levels: of disappointing her mother, of harming her own reputation because she is a good cook. Also, there is an element of investing your time, investing your ability to do things on the spot. If you open phyllo you have to feel it, otherwise you create all these holes in it and your mother or grandmother will laugh at you. And potentially you have to start over from scratch; the more anxious you become because you lose patience, the "bloody thing" feels it, understands it, and acts accordingly because your hands are not smooth, you make jerky movements.[17]

Such reflections resonate with my own observations of the perceived skill and "synesthetic reason" (Paxson 2011) entailed in rolling out phyllo dough. In addition, the symbiotic relationship between the hand, rolling pin, and dough suggests a distributed agency I analyze elsewhere.[18] But here I emphasize the sense of multiple, subjectively perceived dangers, and the rewards that accompany it: the potential to cross the threshold and be considered "good at rolling out a *pitta*." As Pipyrou summarized: "The question is 'who dares to do it?'" Furthermore, one gets a sense of the temporal dimensions of risk-taking, since success involves being able to adjust "on the spot," while also recognizing that one may lose the time invested in the process.

An approach to risk that draws on practice theory and focuses on the everyday rather than the extraordinary gets closer to what I am after. Zinn's book, *Understanding Risk Taking*, largely works in this tradition. Zinn suggests seeing risk and risk-taking as a "normal part of life" (2019: 136), rather than as disruptive or extraordinary. With this approach, "risk-taking appears primarily as part of everyday routines (practices) which constitute risks' mundane character" (2019: 120). According to this view, risk-taking is still dangerous, as much of this work focuses on issues like drug-taking that have strongly negative health or legal consequences. Yet, this practice approach also recognizes that risks are embedded in a larger cultural context of practices within which they make sense. Risks are neither irrational nor rational, as in some of the literature on risk, but rely on tacit knowledge of particular situations. They "are ways of managing uncertainty, and in many circumstances [risk-taking is] more successful than rational strategies" (2019: 278–79). This fits with how I approached Kalymnian cutting as a "technique of the body," as Marcel Mauss would put it, embedded in a specific cultural environment. Kalymnian cutting draws on tacit knowledge to manage the uncertainty of the daily acts of processing and preparing ingredients in which concerns over some objective notion of rationality or efficiency feel highly misplaced.

I am also drawn to work by Giovanni Orlando that explores how the risks associated with eating food produced under conditions of capitalist industrial agriculture are negotiated by consumers in Palermo, Sicily. Rather than experiencing the dangers of food as part of the larger environmental dangers of Beck's "risk society," consumers in Palermo integrate an understanding of food risk into their ordinary lives through what Orlando dubs "risk practice." This "risk practice" played out as much in bodily and sensory experience as in cognitive abstractions about risk posed as top-down, "expert discourses." As Orlando notes, his subjects

> regularly remarked on food's sensorial properties while showing [him] the contents of their kitchen cupboards and fridges, and while actually eating. This synesthetic dimension was linked to notions of risk, as people held the sensual properties of what they ate to be of great significance in establishing which foods were risky and which were not. (2018: 153)

I had similar experiences on Kalymnos, where the risk of cooking was always drawn into local discourses about what makes food "good" and was grounded in Kalymnians' trust for their sensory capacities, as part of a larger "sensory order" (Howes 2003), which I analyze in more detail elsewhere. Kalymnians distinguished between good and bad based on life-long experiences, through which they developed the skills to navigate the myriad challenges of shopping and cooking.[19]

Another useful sense of "objective" risk can be found in Mary Douglas's work. Here, risk is embedded in social and symbolic systems—indeed, much like taboos, ideas about risk help maintain social and political orders. "Risk, in Douglas's view, is the threat of the classificatory system being thrown out of kilter" (Arnoldi 2009: 39). Now we approach a mundane understanding of risk in which it is neither voluntary nor extraordinary, but an inescapable part of everyday perception and action. Douglas developed her ideas of risk and taboo both by exploring the reasons that the ancient Hebrews banned pork (along with many other things), as well as understanding the daily decisions of contemporary life regarding what makes breakfast "breakfast" and dinner "dinner." In this same way, when I was told by Greeks on the island of Kalymnos that carrots don't go in lentil stew, I was confronted with a question of categories and their transgression. I return to Douglas in the context of laying out Sahlins's approach in the next chapter.

But, given these caveats, why use risk at all? At certain points in the following chapters, I will suggest that connected terms such as "contingency," or even "possibility," are appropriate for some aspects of the phenomena I am discussing. Yet, risk provides a convenient term to connect these different levels of analysis, from concerns with the perception of meals and taste to discussions of what is proper and improper cooking. The multiple meanings of risk make my choice of term, *everyday risk,* somewhat risky in itself. It may lead readers to expect certain analytical roads that I will not be traveling. Hopefully, it is a risk that will pay off if I can convince readers that these different ways of thinking about risk are worth their consideration. As Zappa sings "In the kitchen of danger / You can feel like a stranger."[20]

NOTES

1. Counihan 2010; Abarca 2006; Gvion 2012.
2. Weiss 1996; Adapon 2008; Janeja 2010.
3. As I discuss in Sutton 2001: chap. 4.
4. Krishnendu Ray, *New Books in Food*, 31 July 2019, 1:30–1:15 remaining. Retrieved 1 December 2020 from https://podcasts.apple.com/gb/podcast/krishnendu-ray-the-ethnic-restaurateur-bloomsbury-2016/id425670722?i=1000445777418. Even women theorizing often do not seem to have an interest in this topic. As Elisabeth l'Orange Furst (1997: 441) wrote about the tendency to treat woman's cooking as purely an artifact of patriarchal oppression: "Housework [including cooking] in some feminist thinking is considered to be a dull, stupefying, and even slave-like task, and something women ought to be freed from."
5. This was from a Call for Papers for a workshop at University of Oslo organized by Wim Van Daele in 2016 as part of The University of Oslo's European Research Council Overheating Grant, overseen by Thomas Hylland Ericksen.
6. As reviewed in Sutton 2016a.
7. See e.g., Black 2021; Trubek 2017; and Palmié 2013.
8. Pierre Bourdieu's (1990) concepts of habitus and dispositions and Paul Connerton's (1989) of habit memory are two of the most well-known examples of approaches that seek to account for continuity.
9. See Sutton 2011.
10. "Frank Zappa—The Dangerous Kitchen Lyrics," *Songlyrics*. Retrieved 1 December 2020 from http://www.songlyrics.com/frank-zappa/the-dangerous-kitchen-lyrics/.
11. Yoko Akama, Sarah Pink, and Shanti Sumartojo (2018) make a similar argument for the concept of "uncertainty." But unfortunately for my purposes, they seem to want to recuperate uncertainty, to "re-conceptualize uncertainty as generative and inevitable, rather than as threatening" (2018: 25), by separating out its negative aspects as "risk."
12. See discussion in Arnoldi 2009: 51.
13. For a developed critique of Giddens based on her research on changes in a Spanish village, see Jane Collier (1997). For my own contribution to debunking the tradition/modernity dichotomy, see Sutton (1994; 2008).
14. Appadurai 2012; Boholm 2003; Garot 2015; Garsten and Hasselstrom 2003; Palmer 2002.
15. See du Boulay 1974; Sutton 2001: chap. 2.
16. Mintz 1997; Sutton 2014.
17. Pipyrou, personal communication with author via Skype, 25 January 2020. Pipyrou also filmed cooking among some of her friends and neighbors in the village, however her primary field site is in Calabria, Italy (see Pipyrou 2016).
18. See Sutton 2014: chap. 2.
19. See esp. Sutton 2001: chap. 3; Sutton 2014: chap. 1
20. "Frank Zappa—The Dangerous Kitchen Lyrics," *Songlyrics*. Retrieved 1 December 2020 from http://www.songlyrics.com/frank-zappa/the-dangerous-kitchen-lyrics/.

CHAPTER 1

HOW PEOPLE COOK, WHILE THINKING, FOR EXAMPLE

APPROACHING COOKING

In *The Practice of Everyday Life, Volume 2*, Michel de Certeau's colleague Luce Giard develops some thoughts on cooking with structural linguistic metaphors in mind. She writes, "Foodstuffs and dishes are arranged in each [geographic] region according to a detailed code of values, rules, and symbols, around which is organized the alimentary model characteristic of a cultural area in a given period. In this detailed code, more or less well known and followed, the organizer of the family meal will draw on inspiration, on her purchase and preparation possibilities, on her whim and the desires of her 'guests'" (1998: 168). Like de Certeau, Giard is most interested in the practices of cooks, the ways that they negotiate, on a daily basis, the "possibilities" that are afforded by their whims and the desires of their "guests," but still in relation to this shared code. In the conclusion to the book, Giard sums up this notion with the concept of "operativity," by which she suggests: "The art of the cook is all about production, based on a limited choice of available ingredients, in a combination of gestures, proportions, utensils, and cooking or transformation methods" (1998: 254), before turning the metaphor of the linguistic code around and insisting the communication is also a kind of cooking, "*a cuisine of gestures and words* ... with its recipes and its distortions and failures" (1998: 254; emphasis in original). Recipes, once again, suggest a code, while distortions and failures imply the risk undertaken each time one cooks that the result will not match the desired image or may even change it in some way. Giard suggests a validation of "tactics," which are both individual and part of a larger community, that allow the cook to negotiate the myriad challenges and "dangers" of the kitchen with an attentive and "suspicious" eye (1998: 205–6) some of which she bemoans are under assault from the standardization and mechanization processes of modernity, in which the cook's knowledge and skill is replaced by push-buttons and machines that become opaque to the user (1998: 212). I want to address some of these issues raised by skill and deskilling, as well as perception of danger in the kitchen in subsequent chapters. Here I take the notion that cooking involves a code and its instantiations as key to approaching how we might understand it as a micropractice with larger implications, which can open up vistas onto important questions of how continuity is reproduced and how change happens. And for this, I turn to Marshall Sahlins's theory of historical practice.

One of the advantages that the study of cooking offers to the anthropologist is that, as Giard suggested, it is an everyday practice, which, while perhaps "mundane" to some, is never exactly the same from one day to the next. Cooking is always caught up in the contingencies of social situations, changing environments, recalcitrant ingredients, and even ordinary creativity. I will thus be arguing that it lends itself to an understanding of historical process at the micro-level. At the same time, as food scholars have been showing, food is not irrelevant to wider sociopolitical concerns, its mundaneness is also part of its ability to entwine issues of gender, class, race, and identities on multiple scales in the pragmatics of daily life. In this chapter, however, I will focus attention more on the everyday and merely touch on some of the wider issues that may be addressed in this way. My argument is that we can use cooking in dialogue with Sahlins's approach to history in a fruitful manner to develop a way of tracing continuity and change in cooking by deploying Sahlins's notion that we constantly put our categories at risk in practice.

SAHLINS'S THEORY OF HISTORICAL PROCESSES AS THE RISK OF CATEGORIES IN PRACTICE

In discussing the meeting of Captain Cook's crew with Hawaiian women, Sahlins somewhat jokingly writes: "What is for some people a radical event may appear to others as a date for lunch" (1985: 154). My goal in applying Sahlins's thinking to a domain that to my knowledge it has not been thought of previously is to turn this phrase on its head and try to convince readers of the notion that lunch itself, or at least its cooking, might in fact always have the potential to turn into a radical event.

Sahlins's notion of the "risk of categories in practice" develops his model of understanding moments of cultural change, or what he called "the structure of the conjuncture."[1] Sahlins argues, for example, in relation to the way that cultural categories guide perception, that "Man's symbolic hubris becomes a great gamble played with the empirical realities" (1985: 149). Here Sahlins is suggesting that categorization does not automatically cover over inconsistencies, that is, there is always the potential for the world to resist our attempts to fit it into our categories (an idea that Mary Douglas also uses to talk about cultural reactions such as humor, disgust, and taboo as ways of responding to the failure of categories to encompass reality). Here again, Sahlins repeats the metaphor of "gamble" or "risk" in claiming that "meaning is risked in a cosmos fully capable of contradicting the symbolic systems that are presumed to describe it" (1985: 149). Sahlins also argues for "subjective risk" or the notion that historical actors may use categories for their own purposes or as part of their own particular projects, to which the categories, again, may or may not correspond. This is, of course, Sahlins's attempt to resolve the paradox of Structure versus Event that has long bedeviled social science. For Sahlins, Structure and Event are not two separate moments or locations, but rather abstractions of a fundamentally unified reality. Sahlins also contrasts "event," which can potentially alter a system, with "happening," which leaves the system unaffected (e.g., 2005a: 300–3). Historian William Sewell provides a nice summary of Sahlins's position: "In my opinion, Sahlins's theory introduces precisely the right objects of theoretical investigation: structures, which shape the world in their image; events, which, although they are shaped by structures, transform the structures that shaped them; a balky world, which is under no obligation to behave as our categories tell us it should, and subjects, whose interested and creative actions are the human stuff of events" (Sewell 2005: 204). Thus "the event was contingent, but it unfolded in the terms of a particular cultural field, from which the actors drew their reasons and the happening found its meanings" (Sahlins 2004: 291). Cultural continuity, in this view, is the contingent outcome of the play of event and structure, one that may be imposed through processes of memory and interpretation. As Bruce Kapferer notes, "More than a representation of systemic socio-cultural processes, the event is the site for innovative practice and (importantly in Sahlins' work) for the practical construction of cultural memory" (2015: 15).

The "structure of the conjuncture" is Sahlins's third term interposed between structure and event (1985: xiv), that is, the set of interrelationships that makes any "happening" meaningful, or not, by tying it both to the past and to its "specific historical efficacy" (1985: xiv). Elsewhere he refers to it as the dynamics of practice, or "The way the cultural categories are actualized in specific context [sic] through the interested action of the historic agents and the pragmatics of their interaction" (Sahlins, cited in Sewell 2005: 221). Sewell notes that this concept allows Sahlins to point to the fact that "the dy-

namics of events are not utterly chaotic, that they exhibit significant regularities, albeit not the regularities that the actors would have expected. The term
'structure of the conjuncture' is an attempt to signify that the 'conjunctures'
we call events are characterized by emergent regularities or logics and are in
this sense 'structured' in spite of their novelty" (Sewell 2006: 221). Note that
Sewell points here to the emergent aspect of Sahlins's approach to practice,
that he wants to avoid the view that practice simply reproduces structures.
Indeed, Sewell goes on to suggest that it is the "conjuncture of structures" or
the different structures that may be brought into play in any particular situation in novel ways that allows for "novel combinations" (2006: 221), a point
that Sahlins is perhaps not particularly clear on.

Sahlins's approach has been, of course, criticized along a number of lines,
for how it handles the relationship of Westerners and "natives" (Obyesekere
1992), for its model of cognitive processes (Reyna 1997) and for its relatively holistic view of culture (Li 2001), among other things. Sewell draws
extensively from Sahlins's approach to historical process while positing
some caveats as well. In particular, he is concerned that Sahlins emphasizes
one dominant structure at the expense of alternative views or even simply
cultural complexity. As Sewell notes, the association of Hawaiian women
with "tabu" in certain official realms did not discount different definitions of
"woman" in household, agricultural, or interpersonal realms. Or that these
other realms may have their own associated structures (Sewell 2005: 208–
9). Another important question is whether Sahlins's theory overemphasizes
structure at the expense of cultural creativity, which in different ways has
been asserted by some of his major critics as well as those who draw from his
approach. Sewell again notes that "in my opinion Sahlins's account makes
the Hawaiians' crucial and risky acts of reference seem too easy, too automatically generated by the structures in place, and makes Hawaiian actors
seem insufficiently conscious of the risks or reflective about the possibilities of other acts of reference" (2005: 212). Victor Li (2001), in an in-depth
discussion of the Sahlins-Obyesekere debate, comes to similar conclusions,
arguing that despite the dialectical movement between structure and event,
practice is at key moments subordinated to structure in Sahlins's writing.[2]
I will return to these issues below in my consideration of cooking, but for
now, I would note that Sewell clearly argues that these are tensions or problems within Sahlins's approach that do not invalidate the larger project. I
quote his conclusion at length because it captures what he argues is the ongoing value of Sahlins's structural history, along with inserted caveats:

> I argue that events should be conceived of as sequences of occurrences that result in
> transformations of structures. Such sequences begin with a rupture of some kind—
> that is, a surprising break with routine practice. Such breaks actually occur every

day—as a consequence of exogenous causes, of contradictions between structures, of sheer human inventiveness or perversity, or of simple mistakes in enacting routines. But most ruptures are neutralized and reabsorbed into the preexisting structures in one way or another—they may, for example, be forcefully repressed, pointedly ignored, or explained away as exceptions. But whatever the nature of the initial rupture, an occurrence only becomes a historical event, in the sense in which I use the term, when it touches off a chain of occurrences that durably transforms previous structures and practices. (Sewell 2005: 227)

Note how Sewell's summary echoes Douglas as well in the focus on different responses to those events that challenge categories. It is also interesting that Sewell emphasizes the value of this approach for understanding events as "change" or "rupture," although presumably this approach could also help us understand the "happenings" that did not rise to the level of events, or ruptures, and seemed, subjectively or objectively, to simply reproduce things as they are. This, too, of course, requires interpretive work, as the possibility to recognize something as similar, or simply to ignore it as part of the flow of the familiar, is very much part of the work of daily life that anthropologists have become increasingly interested in. Robin Wagner-Pacifici also emphasizes ruptures as key in her challengingly titled book *What Is an Event?* Indeed, she sees happenings such as births, deaths, and large-scale violence as prototypical candidates for ruptures that become events, while much of what I am interested in here, the everyday, would be seen in her formula as "ground." However, she also explores the ambiguities between rupture and ground, and the way that events may change shape, or form, over time, suggesting that: "Events are restless. Identities can come and go; our ability to see them depends on the forms in which they appear, the affordances of those forms, and the forces that interrogate and combine the forms" (Wagner-Pacifici 2017: 113). The notion that events take, or fail to take, particular forms and that these forms may afford certain possibilities, I think is useful in thinking about why certain happenings may eventually become events, whether at the loud, public end of things or at the quotidian and ordinary end.

So the concept of "rupture" may not be as useful to us given that it prejudges certain events as "surprising" in order to be marked as interesting. John Comaroff also tends to define rupture as "the unexpected, the counterintuitive" and points to "theatrical moments of rupture" as a useful methodological stratagem (2010: 531). I do not doubt that anthropologists may profitably use the surprising as a key part of our toolkit and our project of "critical estrangement" (2010: 531). However, the value of Sahlins's approach seems to me that it gives us a way of thinking about reproduction as well as change, indeed it poses the two as fundamentally inseparable. And furthermore, we will see that in examining Greek cooking it might be better to think of the potential for imagining everyday ruptures, or risks, as a built-in feature of the cooking environment, rather than seeing rupture as necessarily a loud break from the familiar.

Approaches from sociological practice theory no doubt could also be relevant to these questions. If I had begun with Pierre Bourdieu, rather than Sahlins, perhaps I would not need to bring in Tim Ingold's insights on the mutual construction of people and their material environments and embodiments, as I do in chapter 2. I find however, that Bourdieu gives us more of a sense of micropractices from the point of view of stability and continuity rather than change. Other practice theorists address change directly. Elizabeth Shove, Mika Pantzar, and Matt Watson (2012), for example, develop an approach to tracing changing practices they divide into three aspects: "materials," "competencies," and "meanings" to trace their circulation and reproduction together as a bundle and as separate elements. Alan Warde in his book-length (2016) discussion of the implications of practice theory for food studies, uses similar terms: "procedures," "shared understandings," and the sedimentation of a "practical sense" or disposition that generates food practices. He also notes the "knock-on effects" of adjacent practices in potentially generating change (2016: 134). I get the sense, however, that these theorists tend to analytically separate change from continuity. What Sahlins's approach offers that I think is particularly useful in understanding cooking is, as I have been arguing, the idea that change and continuity are always necessarily aspects of the same process. At the end of the day, of course, everyone chooses a vocabulary that makes them comfortable, which has its strengths and weaknesses. While I leave the fuller implications of other "practice theories" to an approach to cooking for future consideration, I would note that missing from many of these approaches is an explicit focus on risk or contingency, and it is this aspect that I find critical for understanding cooking.

RISKY CATEGORIES AND "CULTURE"

In some ways, Sahlins's approach could be seen as derived from what is anthropological common sense on the significance of "culture" as schemata that organize perception, as Sahlins likes to cite Boas: "The seeing eye [is] the organ of tradition" (Sahlins 2005a: 152).

If Sahlins's theory is very much in line with dominant anthropological understandings, it is interesting to note that very little ethnographic work on history seems to draw explicitly on a Sahlinsian approach to historical process.[3] That is, recent anthropology does not seem to explicitly address processes of change—or continuity, for that matter—by drawing on Sahlins's model. Much of recent work on "history" in anthropology, indeed seems more interested in questions of "historicity" or "historical consciousness"—

that is, the ways people's understandings of the past are shaped by culturally specific temporalities, as well as by things like kinship, ritual practice, and power—rather than in questions of historical process.[4] Others that focus explicitly on change do so by examining a "before" and "after" without positing their studies ethnographically in the moment of change. For example, Jane Collier's magisterial book *From Duty to Desire* (1997) looks at the ways people conceptualize their agency in a Spanish village over a twenty-five-year period. She examines changing discourses of "duty" and "desire" as explanations for the choices people make. But in an otherwise rich and thoughtful ethnography, Collier does not show us with any extended ethnography how this change took place.

The Manchester School, led by Max Gluckman, was an exception in this regard, in its focus on events they saw as potentially transformative. As Kapferer notes, "it was events that broke the apparent calm or routine of everyday life that were the focus of Gluckman's Manchester anthropology" (Kapferer 2015: 3). While Gluckman's approach tended to focus on Political events (with a capital "P") that challenged the sociopolitical system, he also pointed anthropological attention to under-the-surface tensions that led to "moments in which the intransigencies and irresolvable tensions ingrained in social and personal life . . . boiled to the surface and became, if only momentarily, part of public awareness for the participants as well as for the anthropologist" (Kapferer 2015: 3).

RISKY MOUSSAKA AND OTHER METAPHORS

Sahlins's theory, then, has clear relevance to cooking in that it provides one handle on how to understand continuity and change at the micro-level of everyday cooking practices, which I turn to now.

Let's take a concrete example of cooking something—let's say moussaka. Reserved typically for a Sunday meal on Kalymnos, moussaka is an elaborate dish of layered potatoes and eggplant with ground meat and a béchamel sauce on top. In making moussaka, that category is put at risk as a multitude of contingencies come into play in determining the eventual outcome of the dish. What if one is short on time, or eggs, and decides to substitute a packaged béchamel for the homemade version? There is also the question of what meat to use. On Kalymnos some people make it with beef and some with a mixture of beef and pork. The latter is seen by some as cheaper (ground pork is typically somewhat cheaper than ground beef), but for some it is also more flavorful. Ground lamb is unusual on Kalymnos, though it is used in other parts of Greece where lamb is more available. Some Kalymnians told me that it was simply not a choice because of availability, while others said that the idea of moussaka with lamb was "disgusting!" While veal is not typical on Kalymnos (but found elsewhere), I was told by some that it would likely be tasty (but they hadn't tried it). All of these variations can potentially be absorbed into the category "moussaka," but also might call for adjustments. If one were to make it with ground lamb, one might have to append "moussaka with lamb" to the name of the dish, while others would simply reject that as a possibility, or maybe would absorb it into the concept of "what some other Greeks do." Another way to phrase this is to think of the dish, or the recipe, as a kind of abstract "form" in Wagner-Pacifici's terms, which may help to contain a particular meal as a recognizable event rather than simply a chaotic mess of ingredients. How much change, how many missing or substituted ingredients could still be fit into the form of the dish before it became unrecognizable as such and would have to either be contained in a different form ("something thrown together," perhaps, or "a failure"), or be absorbed without notice into the stream of daily meals.

And this is just at the level of ingredients, a whole other set of contingencies may arise in the cooking process itself. There is a proper procedure and order, at least for some, in adding spices to the tomato sauce the meat cooks in. Cooks might make a change midstream as they decide they want to make the recipe "lighter" or with less salt for health reasons.[5] A historical change is the increasing number of people who cook the vegetables (eggplant, potato) in the oven rather than frying them to use less oil in the dish. Some substitute margarine for butter in the process, which is believed by many to be healthier. But all of these changes are seen as "less traditional moussaka." Some may like to include nutmeg, while others do not because of the flavor or because they think it is not a traditional ingredient.[6] And of course, a perfectly executed, delicious moussaka would be an abomination if served during the wrong time, Easter Week for instance, when most Greeks are expected to be fasting. All of these contingencies (and many more) ensure that no moussaka is exactly the same as any other. So far, this much is perhaps obvious. But what happens as each contingency is incorporated into the dish "moussaka"? One can say that it is likely that on a typical day these small changes may not be particularly noticeable, though on Kalymnos, where conversation about meals is a constant accompaniment to eating, changes are more noticeable than those with a less-trained palate might think.[7] So, ordinary contingencies might remain at the level of happenings, but they also have the potential to stretch the category moussaka, since something that looks or tastes slightly different is eaten under the label "moussaka." This is what Sahlins refers to as the "great gamble with empirical realities" as the label insists on continuity, while practice will always produce some change. It does not matter for my purposes whether the change is intentional or unintentional. The cook might stir the béchamel sauce into the casserole rather

than keeping it as a separate layer on top because of fears that it would otherwise overflow the pan, as one Kalymnian woman described to me. Or one
might make it without noting any differences in practice, but it still might
turn out tasting "not right." One might use ground pork instead of beef or
lamb, in which case, the response might be on the one hand a clear rejection—"that's not moussaka!"—with the rejection being based on taste or tradition or both. Or it could be a discovery—"that's different, but really good!"
All of these examples fit with the model being developed here, although
perhaps the first example, deciding to make it with lamb, is somewhat different in that it could begin with an alteration of the label: "moussaka with
lamb." However, the results are all similar in that in each case the category
is potentially altered. To quote Sahlins: "Every reproduction of culture is an
alteration, insofar as in action, the categories pick up some novel empirical
content" (1985: 144). In this case we can say that every dish is like moussaka,
that is, every dish might potentially pick up novel empirical content while
still very likely reproducing the category as the label "moussaka" is not typically rejected and replaced with something else.

I want to highlight the example of stirring in the béchamel sauce rather
than simply pouring it on top. Here is something that has been essential to
the definition of moussaka for a long time on Kalymnos. However, when one
of my informants mentioned this innovation, she still thought of it as making
"moussaka," but the result was strikingly different in the overall look and
texture of the dish. She said she had not planned this innovation; rather she
had come upon it when she had made too much béchamel and was afraid it
was going to spill out of the pan, so she stirred it to allow some to sink down
in the pan. In describing this to me and to her neighbor, she illustrated the
stirring motion by grabbing what was nearest to hand, a paintbrush and a
roll of tape, and mimicking how she would do it with a real moussaka. The
advantage, she said, of this technique was that it allowed the flavor of the
béchamel to pervade the entire dish, rather than having the béchamel sit like
a "brick" on top of the rest. It was the kind of change that some of her neighbors might say is "no longer moussaka," because it is not simply a matter of
altered ingredients within a range of possibilities, but rather a change in the
basic look or structure of the dish (even if the ingredients are all the same).
Indeed, one Athenian informant that I asked about this version of moussaka responded concisely that it "would not be a moussaka. One of the key
things in moussakas is the layering of the ingredients." The question, then,
is: will she continue to make this dish, and will it change, or simply expand
the category?

In the vast majority of cases, of course, any small alteration in a recipe
would not constitute an "event" in the language of Sahlins and Sewell in that
it could simply be ignored or forgotten. In Mary Douglas's sense, it could be

rejected as "disgusting" or funny, as with the "moussaka with lamb" or when a Kalymnian woman who had lived in Australia attempted to cook stew with meat that hadn't been defrosted and was met with derision by her neighbors. In such cases, the category dominates, and the empirical risk is rejected whole hog. But other categories may be more inherently flexible. And what is interesting is the implication of Sahlins's approach that in many cases the category itself will expand to accommodate the new empirical content. I am interested in the cumulative effects of such a shift: how a recipe might be altered to accommodate new ingredients, techniques, or flavors at the same time it is seemingly reproduced, both rupture and reproduction. To stick with moussaka for a moment, it was only in the 1990s that preprepared béchamel sauce became available on Kalymnos. Now suddenly Kalymnian cooks had to choose whether they would make béchamel themselves or buy it at the store, and whether the latter would still count as "real" moussaka. Since béchamel is time consuming to make, it also afforded some people who didn't make moussaka in the past the possibility of making it, but perhaps feeling that it was not authentic. The same thing can be traced for items like phyllo dough to make various Greek pies (cheese pie, spinach pie, etc.). Although in that case, making pies was uncommon on Kalymnos before the 1980s, pies being seen as more of a mainland dish, so there was less of a "tradition" to displace. These cases clearly bring in larger issues and moral dimensions because choices such as these—especially in a largely face-to-face community such as Kalymnos—are not made by individuals acting alone, but in relation to families and communities, as I describe in my ethnography of Kalymnian cooking (Sutton 2014: chap. 1). They are still weighted with moral dimensions as to "proper" food and often "proper" gender behavior as well. However, I think that a focus on the subtler changes discussed above can be illuminating because they can illustrate how change happens in less obvious ways.

In the example of a new technique for béchamel sauce I am pointing to one type of change that Sewell points us to: endogenous creativity. In this case, the woman literally came upon this technique as she tried to solve a problem in the midst of cooking. However, the approach I am suggesting works equally well for exploring other types of change: "exogenous causes and contradictions between structures." Exogenous causes would include new ingredients made available from various sources as well as the influence of restaurant food, TV cooking shows, return migrants, and the internet.[8] Of course, the distinction between "endogenous" and "exogenous" is always provisional, as we well know that one can become the other very easily with historical perspective, not to mention the fact of our growing understanding of our inherent otherness as revealed by everything from the remains of retroviruses in our DNA to the microbiome we each carry with us, indeed we all "contain multitudes" (Yong 2016).

So endogenous and exogenous are always provisional and perspectival categories. In my moussaka example, it was the introduction of a "new," though familiar, ingredient, the packaged béchamel sauce that potentially caused a change in cooking practice. Similarly, contradictions in structures can be illustrated through this example as Kalymnians balance competing imperatives in cooking: taste, health, care, convenience, gender conformity, independence, and creativity.[9] All of these structures are often explicit in Kalymnian cooking discourses, and cooks develop various strategies for managing their potentially contradictory implications on daily cooking practice. However, as researchers I would suggest that we should also be attuned to changes that, at least at first, may go unnoticed by our informants, and which may have larger impacts down the road. That would attune us to examples of risk of categories that Sahlins suggests happens even when people may explicitly deny any change and attempt to recuperate all practice as simply reproduction of "tradition."

A few suggestive ethnographic studies of food have pointed to some of the ways one might think about the development of recipes within a broader notion of cuisine, or style, and how continuity and change might work at these larger levels. Richard Wilk (2006: 112–23) looks specifically at a number of examples of how ingredients specifically culturally marked as "foreign" are incorporated into Belizean cooking in terms of the notion of "creolization." His approach is meant to specify some of the ways that creolization occurs, so that ingredients and techniques are not simply mixed together, they may be incorporated through a wide range of processes that he specifies as blending, submersion, substitution, wrapping and stuffing, compression, and alternation and promotion. Submersion, for example, is the mixing in of a foreign ingredient so that it becomes indistinguishable in the finished dish (for example, bouillon cubes). Substitution often takes the form of swapping out a new, but often similar, ingredient in a familiar recipe. Wrapping and stuffing is the process by which foreign ingredients are covered by a familiar package, a tortilla or white sandwich bread, for example. In the case of Belize, such processes could work in both directions, as a colonial cuisine could substitute local ingredients for "familiar" English dishes, such as *callaloo*, in which a Belizean leafy green substituted for European spinach (and was indeed called spinach) (Wilk 2006: 117).

Stephan Palmié's suggestively titled *The Cooking of History* (2013) leans more heavily on the metaphorical dimensions of certain foods and attendant cooking processes to think about questions of creolization and hybridity of religion and of history itself in Cuba. He uses cooking as a metaphor for transformation, but one in which ingredients can be more or less transformed, remain more or less recognizable in the process. For example, he picks up on the Cuban scholar Fenando Ortiz's comparison of Cuban identity and history to an *ajiaco*, a stew. But not one that mixes ingredients indistinguishably together as in the metaphor of the melting pot (which is not, of course, a culinary metaphor at all), but one that captures both the synchronic and dia-chronic mixing of ingredients in various states of transformation. Ortiz compares Cuban history to an "incessant bubbling of heterogeneous substances... [that] has a different flavor and consistency depending on whether one tastes what is at the bottom, in the middle, or at its top, where the viandas are still raw, and the bubbling liquid still clear" (Ortiz, cited in Palmié 2013: 98). As Palmié notes: "As novel ingredients sink to stratigraphically lower lev-els, their relative cooking time increases, 'transculturating' them to stages or phases of cubanidad [Cubanness] already achieved by prior ingredients that have partly lost their recognizable 'extraneousness' by blending in with others" (2013: 99).[10] Palmié develops these ideas as part of a never-ending "cooking" process in Cuban scholarship and identity and as part of his cri-tique of objectified notions of culture that can be found both in scholars that focus on African "survivals" and in those that argue for a more static notion of hybridity. In other words, just as cookbook authors often do, scholars, including anthropologists, often fall into the error of objectifying and en-textualizing more fluid culinary and other cultural practices (2013: 224).[11] But he also cites Sahlins's approach to historical change, and notes that we need to focus on particular structures of the conjuncture to understand how "existing collective representations pick up novel content, and novel repre-sentations are launched into collective circulation" (2013: 54). He develops these extended metaphors in looking at the different histories and suggestive meanings (in terms of African derivation or New World creation/recreation) in iconic dishes like the Jamaican ackee and saltfish and the Cuban amalá con quimbombó (2013: 226–28).[12]

Both Wilk's and Palmié's approaches are much more on the macro-level than what is being argued for here. The obvious advantage of these ap-proaches—somewhat more metaphorical in Palmié's case—is that they relate these processes of culinary transformation to larger questions about creolized identities and colonialism. For my purposes, however, while highly sugges-tive, they do not show the micro-process of change in action as I have been proposing. They do, however, allow us to think of some of the ways diverse "events" could be incorporated into structures through particular forms (rec-ipes of different kinds). Thus, their approaches are in some ways the other side of Mary Douglas's argument about ways of rejecting unfamiliar elements or things that challenge categories. Instead of showing their rejection, Wilk provides a template for some of the different ways the unfamiliar (ingredient, technique, or even meal temporality[13]) can be incorporated and at the same time expand categories/recipes, while Palmié suggests more broadly that historical transformations can in fact work like cooking.

Joy Adapon (2008) takes a different approach to understanding the transformation of recipes in her field site of Milpa Alta, Mexico. Drawing on
Alfred Gell's approach to artwork and agency, developed throughout her
ethnography, Adapon argues that a recipe might be imagined to be like a
person that has relationships with other persons: "it can 'marry' and 'have
offspring' and thus forms a lineage. Conceived of in this way, there are ex-
tensive families of recipes . . . Some of these are related to each other; others
seem to have nothing to do with one another as they are completely different and do not mix" (2008: 103). Of course, it might stay proudly single as
well. Adapon illustrates the concept of a recipe lineage with the example of
the development of salsa recipes from "simple" to "complex." She illustrates
points where, in her tree diagram, a recipe can still be thought of as "the
same" but have a variety of ingredients, and other points where the addition
of an ingredient makes it branch into something else—from pico de gallo,
for example, to guacamole—"although chili is no longer the main ingredient
of the salsa called guacamole, it can still be seen as a precursor to the development of the recipe" (2008: 103). Adapon goes on to suggest similar sche-
matic diagrams for the relationship of different recipes within a "cuisine,"
suggesting that traditional cuisines develop "as spatio-temporal wholes,"
once again drawing from Gell's notion of "style" in the artwork of a community (2008: 105). Rather than focusing on the specific types of interactions of
"foreign" and "indigenous" ingredients developed by Wilk, Adapon suggests
that transformations be seen in terms of "modifications," "offshoots," and
"innovations" to capture the different interrelations between one recipe and
another (2008: 108).

Adapon makes the important point, perhaps not made explicit in my argument above, that recipes—like all "traditional art"—develop and "are refined" by a community of interacting individuals who influence each other's
cooking styles,[14] and who display skill in using ingredients, tools, and techniques, the latter point will be developed in the next chapter. She suggests,
though does not elaborate in her ethnography, the relationship of the "style"
of a cuisine with Nancy Munn's notion of "value transformations" that suggest that culinary styles may interpenetrate with other "levels of meaning in
social life" (2008: 105). She thus implies, as Wilk does more explicitly, how
the study of cooking and its transformations may shed important insights
onto other cultural domains or questions of power.

Adapon sums up her analysis as follows:

> I may learn to make salsa with tomatoes, onions, green chile and salt, and then to-
> morrow try out using dried chiles, or a combination of chiles, or add garlic, to make
> another salsa that still tastes as Mexican as the salsa that I first learned to make. If the
> salsa is successful, I may take note and repeat what I have done on another occasion,

and eventually this may become a regular part of my recipe repertoire . . . Innovation, therefore, may be planned or can happen by accident, yet as much as there is innovation and change, there is also repetition and constancy. (2008: 106)

Although Adapon does not provide specific ethnography to show how such transformations and repetitions might occur, she suggests a model very much in line with the Sahlins/Sewell approach. Her innovation comes through focusing specifically on ingredients and their interrelation as part of a larger "style," which fits with her model drawn from Gell and associated notions of nonhuman agency. She suggests here that change is not purely random, but that it shows development based on a hierarchy of ingredients, flavors, and their interrelations. This is important insofar as it suggests to me that Sahlins's model needs to be modified to take into account the materiality of the elements (ingredients), rather than seeing them, in Saussurian fashion, as strictly arbitrary, they can be "motivated" by flavor interrelationships and other sensory properties, all of which add up to a particular cultural "style." Despite this, the quote suggests once again that attention to the material and sensory does not invalidate Sahlins's model of change or the notion of the "risk of categories in practice." Indeed, it makes it more powerful.

MICRO-ETHNOGRAPHY AND MACRO-CHANGE

One possible objection to my argument concerns the relevance of tracing changes in everyday cooking practices and recipes. Or, in other words, is a new way of making moussaka too insignificant for the larger claims that I have been putting forth about risk, continuity, and change? Indeed, a recent discussion between anthropologist Christina Toren and philosopher of science Tim Lewens raised this concern for me quite trenchantly.[15] Lewens was discussing the analogies and dis-analogies between organic and cultural evolution and used the example of a recipe for kedgeree.[16] He noted that for all sorts of reasons from conscious intention to accident, he might change the recipe for kedgeree slightly, and if the result was deemed successful that change might survive to the next generation. This was used as an example of the general point that mathematical evolutionary models can be designed to show the impact of social learning on transmission of kedgeree or presumably other cultural elements. Lewens suggests a "marketplace" of beliefs, skills, and other cultural elements that people may be drawn to reproduce or not to reproduce from one generation to the next.[17] One can imagine what an anthropologist might think of the assumptions behind such a view. Toren's response was that what "evolves" is a "life-cycle," and kedgeree making is "not interesting." We could track all the changes in kedgeree, but what is

missing from that analysis would be all of the ways that the production, exchange, and consumption of food is embedded in a total system of life.[18] Toren concluded that to talk about changes in kedgeree outside of this context
is to "leech the thing of everything that's interesting about it."

It is certainly true that tracing "cultural elements" has long been out of
favor among sociocultural anthropologists. It represents a focus more associated with "evolutionary" sociobiology (Barkow, Cosmides, and Tooby
1995). Within anthropology, Dan Sperber (1996) offers an "epidemiological
approach" to culture as a set of elements, and Greg Urban (2001) comes close
to seeing culture as a set of "memes" in his tracking of the success and failure
of the transmission of cultural elements such as the movie *Dr. Strangelove.*
But the problem with all of these approaches from a broader anthropological perspective is not their interest in specific cultural "elements," surely
something that all anthropologists share, but their tendency to treat these
elements in isolation from the broader society in which they occur, as if
the whole is no more than the sum of its parts.[19] Karin Barber provides a
somewhat sympathetic discussion of Sperber's and Urban's approaches, but
notes, similarly to Toren:

> Human populations become mere carriers of cultural elements which move, mutate,
> colonize new territory and propagate themselves, and whose success or otherwise
> is ascribed to their inherent properties rather than to what human beings decide to
> do with them . . . The human effort to make things stick has dropped from view—
> and with it, history, intertextuality, genre and the collective creation that happens
> between people and exceeds the sum of their individual representations. (2007: 36)[20]

In other words, in our interest to focus on change, or ruptures, as noted
above, we have tended to leave behind questions of how *continuity* happens,
as an active, sociocultural process with risk and change built-in that keeps in
view the micropractices of everyday life and techniques of the body. Without clearly addressing these issues, we have perhaps left them to evolutionary psychologists like Lewens and a few mavericks outside of mainstream of
anthropology.

Part of the struggle of food studies since its growth in the late 1990s has
been to show its broader relevance to other areas of scholarly interest, or
in other words, that kedgeree is not just kedgeree. In the same way, in my
discussion of Wilk and Adapon, I suggested some of the ways that an interest in recipes and their transformations might be tied to other dimensions
of culture. Often continuities and changes in food practices and in tastes
are related to issues in society such as individuation or homogenization,
changing (and reproducing) gender, racial, or ethnic identities, although the
arrow of causality is generally seen as going from these "larger" issues to
food practices, without a sense of the dialectic between the two. One might,

for example, try to trace the change on Kalymnos over the past thirty years from potatoes cooked with meat and sauce to potatoes cooked separately, usually as french fries, with the influence of restaurants and of the younger generation on cooking practices.[21] At what point did the cooks on Kalymnos, mainly older women,[22] decide, or were persuaded, not to reproduce potatoes cooked with sauce, and to substitute french fries on a repeated basis? I am not opposed to tracing the relationship of these larger influences to the daily practices of cooking. Rather I am suggesting that by studying cooking in the way I am suggesting, as a daily "risk" that both reproduces and changes recipes and practices on the micro-level, we can better understand how some of these "larger" changes or reproductions happen in their granularity.

This is, once again, an approach that I would tie to Sahlins—though certainly not exclusively—in his writings on micro- and macro-histories (e.g., 2005b). He poses this as the problem of "how small issues are turned into Big Events" (2005b: 6), which he explores through a number of examples including the "iconization" of Elian Gonzalez—the boy from Cuba who washed up in Florida and became a cause célèbre for the Miami Cuban community and an important, possibly determinative incident in the 2000 presidential election. He also explores the local factionalisms that were part of the Peloponnesian wars as described by Thucydides. He is particularly interested in the "structural relays" or the ways that "Higher-level oppositions are interpolated in lower-level conflicts and vice-versa" (2005b: 6). He explores this process on the one hand in terms of symbolic analogies. So, for example, a local conflict is heightened through a "motivated ideological inflation: namely, poor brother is to rich brother as the common people are to the plutocrats" (2005b: 16). On the other hand, he stresses the role of particular social structures that make certain connections possible, such as the segmentary relations of the polis in ancient Athens and Sparta (which he compares to E. E. Evans-Pritchard's segmentary lineages), which makes it easier to project lower-level conflicts onto higher levels and vice versa: "More complex struggles, for example the *stasis* at Corcyra and the Elian affair, are constituted by superimposing or redoubling the same elementary form at higher levels of order" (2005b: 25).

While focused on conflict here, this is an elaboration of Sahlins's notion of the "structure of the conjuncture" applied more broadly. In my own work on Kalymnos, I explored the numerous ways that people use "analogic thinking" to tie local and national experience in the realms of politics, history, and everyday life (Sutton 1998).[23] Nosy neighbors would casually be compared with the spying activities of "neighboring" countries, and a brutal husband to the Turkish invasion of Cyprus. It is these kinds of metaphorical connections that people use to relate throwing yoghurt at politicians to their critique of neoliberal austerity (Vournelis 2013) that allow one Kalymnian woman to tie the choice of a can opener to family conflicts over who is "traditional" and who is "modern," and the offer of a bag of fruit from a friend to the "solidarity movement" that has developed in Greece since the financial crisis. In thinking about social structural elements that might make small cooking events into large ones it would be important to look at a number of factors. These include the growing influence of restaurant food and return migrants on Kalymnian cooking practices, the identification of many urban residents with the rural villages of their family origins (Papacharalampous 2019) and competitiveness between villages and islands throughout Greece. One could also look at the ways food TV in Greece has promoted local cooking variations onto a national stage, such as the presentation of the Kalymnian variation of stuffed grape leaves on the hugely popular show *Forgiveness with Every Bite*[24] or the appearance of a popular Kalymnian contestant on the Greek version of Master Chef in 2019. Of course, these complex interactions remind us of Sewell's point that there is not a singular "structure of the conjuncture" that we need to attend to, but rather, a "conjunction of structures" (Steinmetz 2008: 541–42).

CONCLUSION

In this chapter I have been aiming to use Marshall Sahlins's understanding of history as "the risk of categories in practice" to raise issues of continuity and change in cooking and recipes, whether or not *risk* is particularly salient in any particular local discourse about cooking. Second, I have suggested that Sahlins's theory of history, with certain modifications, deserves another look for those who want to understand micro-historical processes, and that this might be a useful way to start in the understanding of larger processes as well. Rather than just positing abstract forces like "globalization" or "neoliberalism" and tracking their impacts "before" and "after," we should also try and understand how change happens. With that starting point, I would suggest that the neglected concept in Sahlins's approach of "the risk of categories in practice" might be useful. Finally, I have been making a case here for cooking not simply as an ethnographic topic, but for its relevance to our theoretical understanding. This is specifically because it is a practice that happens typically on a daily basis and thus potentially offers us unusual ethnographic access to how culture is reproduced/altered in each of its iterations (while still allowing us to focus on how this particular "element" of culture is embedded in a much wider and also changing/ reproducing context). Palmié's grand metaphor, the "cooking of history," is helpful here. He uses metaphor in talking of cooking, while also at times relying on metonym to fill out his analogies and at times on historical tracing of ingredients and techniques. In the end, he suggests that ackee and saltfish and amalá con quimbombó are models of and models for a historical reality, "metahistorical instructions for organizing and representing a past the 'reality' of which ultimately remains within discourse," and which can never be known objectively (2013: 250). In this chapter I have not used specific dishes as prototypes or models, but rather suggested that by going deeper into the everyday life of kitchens, meals, and the (mostly) women who cook them, we can use the continuity and change of these familiar and quotidian dishes as a model of (and for) historical processes that we wish to understand, as a testing ground for a theory of history derived (mostly) from Sahlins, which puts everyday risk at its center.

Returning to Giard's initial ethnography of cooking, I noted that while she points us in the direction of a Sahlinsian analysis of categories, she is also concerned with risk as a component of cooking skill, the "operativity" of creative practice that she sees as a key aspect of resistance to the deadening homogenization of technological modernity. In the next chapter I will explore this second aspect of risk in everyday cooking in order to expand the notion that risk is a rubric through which to understand "what is cooking" and to build a theory of cooking. I will examine the question of how people (mostly women) deploy skill in facing the contingencies of the contemporary kitchen environment.

NOTES

1. As noted by Alex Golub, Daniel Rosenblatt, and John Kelly (2016: 17), Sahlins derived the structure of the conjuncture from Fernand Braudel, but transformed Braudel's focus on structures of the *longue durée,* which were only changed by major, often technological discoveries. Instead, Sahlins emphasized different types of structures and their associated temporalities in play at any particular moment: "Sahlins borrowed the Annales sense of history as a conjuncture of different temporal rhythms to replace a layer-cake model with an image of intersecting, multiply paced causal forces that combine in unpredictable ways."
2. As Victor Li puts it, "'Practice of the structure' involves the instantiation or putting into play and into risk of cultural structures or concepts, while 'structure of the practice' requires that the unforeseen and new elements ushered in by practice be reconceptualized as part of a cultural structure. In either case, however, practice, though dialectically related, appears also to be subordinate to structure" (2001: 241–42). See also Jonathan Friedman (1988).
3. Golub et al. (2016) are a recent exception. See, especially, Joel Robbins's (2016) contribution to that collection.
4. Carsten 2007; Hirsch and Stewart 2005; Stewart 2016; Zeitlyn 2015.
5. See Sutton 2014: 153–55.
6. See Sutton 2014: 166.

7. See Sutton 2001: chap. 4; 2014: chap. 1 on Kalymnian conversations about the taste of food.
8. I have given attention to a number of these sources of influence on Kalymnian cooking in Sutton 2014. I do not want to overemphasize the contrast between "endogenous" and "exogenous," as these simply represent moments in time. As historians and anthropologists well know, even the most familiar ingredients were at one point "exogenous."
9. See Sutton 2014: chap. 6.
10. In commenting on Palmié's book, Margaret Weiner notes that different processes of cooking might give rise (fortuitously?) to different understandings of history. In Bali, she notes, both cooking and history are "rhizomatic" involving pounding rather than stewing as the key transformative process (2015: 539).
11. See also Meredith Abarca's (2017: 29–31) concept of "transculinary affirmations," which she uses to discuss some of the ways that African tastes and food memories are incorporated into the preparation of new, yet familiar ingredients such as cassava in encounters with Amerindian and other influences in Latin countries. I discuss Abarca's concept further in chapter 3.
12. Ackee and saltfish represent less hybridity than New World creation, following the historical approach to the Caribbean of Sidney Mintz and Richard Price (1992). Amalá con quimbombó on the surface seems to represent a more Africanist perspective, but Palmié argues that it ultimately shows the impossibility of ever completely and satisfactorily assigning origins or ownership of diverse and shifting historical and cultural elements.
13. For example, "alternation and promotion" is how Richard Wilk describes some of the ways that foreign foods enter the Belizean diet as "snacks," in other words, on a different rhythm than the standard Belizean meal.
14. I explore the notion of influence in cooking techniques, styles, and recipes in Sutton 2014: chap. 5
15. *LSE: Public Lectures and Events*, "Darwinism and the Social Sciences," 29 February 2016. Retrieved 12 January 2020 from https://itunes.apple.com/us/podcast/london-school-economics-public/id279428154?mt=2&i=364014085. Lewens's discussion runs from roughly 34 min in. Toren's response is at 43 min.
16. A popular breakfast dish in England deriving from India containing fish, rice, eggs, and various seasonings.
17. A recent version of this approach, which is more informed by sociocultural anthropology than most, can be found in H. A. Heinrich and V. Weiland (2016).
18. See Christina Toren (2001) for how this fit into her larger approach.
19. Urban modifies this approach in his later work (see Urban 2010).
20. See also Ellen and Fischer 2013.
21. French fries existed on Kalymnos in the past, but were associated with specific dishes, such as french fries and boiled greens or french fries cooked with fried eggs. They were much less frequent as part of the main daily meal.
22. As I discuss (Sutton 2014: chap. 4), women tend to hold onto the power of cooking into their old age, even depriving the "privilege" of making daily cooking decisions from their older married daughters.
23. For example, I explore the relationship of local naming practices to understandings of the international political controversy over the name "Macedonia." Of course, there is nothing particularly new in this insight, and anthropologists have long been

making claims for the wider relevance of their particular, often offbeat examples. For a review of anthropological use of examples, see Bruce Kapferer (2015) and Lars Hojer and Andreas Bandak (2015).

24. See the discussion of this in Sutton 2014: chap. 5. Of course it was not the single Kalymnian variation of stuffed grape leaves (filla) but rather one particular Kalymnian woman's interpretation of the Kalymnian recipe that provoked considerable discussion at the time.

CHAPTER 2

"THAT'S NOT COOKING!"
Human Creativity or
Mechanical Reproduction?

In the previous chapter, I laid out what a theory of cooking might look like if we take "the risk of categories in practice" as our central theme. This risk could in large part be seen as a conceptual matter, that is, what is risked is the idea of dishes and flavors, even if the manifestation of these dishes and flavors are very much material. That is, Sahlins's approach helps us understand how we think about cooking, and how that thinking might change as we actually cook. But it is less interested in the actual execution of that cooking, aspects of which may not have anything to do with categories and linguistic meanings, but rather might be about how we hold a knife and use it to chop an onion, most of the time relatively unconsciously. And there is certainly risk involved in that, as well!

In this chapter, then, I take a different approach to cooking as risk, one that focuses on the skilled, bodily practice involved in cooking. This is what Luce Giard (1998: 205) refers to as the "parrying gestures" such as knowing how to "flatten half cooked fish in order to remove the deadly bones" but also knowing how to improvise "when fresh milk 'turns' on the stove, when meat taken out of the package and trimmed of fat, reveals itself to be not enough to feed four guests, or when Matthieu brings a little friend to dinner unannounced and one has to make the leftover stew 'go a little farther.'" These are the tactics that each cook has internalized to face daily dangers in the kitchen, which are as much social and sensory as they are material. This skilled practice can also be seen as a kind of risk, one identified by craft theorist David Pye (1968, 1969) as "the workmanship of risk" in a fifty-year-old phrase that continues to be cited today by those exploring the embodied and sensory intricacies of craft practice. "In the workmanship of risk, 'the quality of the result is not predetermined, but depends on the judgment, care and dexterity which the maker exercises as he works'" (cited in Adamson 2013: 73). Pye imagined a continuum on which the workmanship of risk was at one end, and the "workmanship of certainty" on the other. The workmanship of certainty, then, involved processes of making where risk had been largely removed, typically by mechanical means. The opposition, then, broadly suggests the distinction between "homemade," "by hand" or "DIY" processes on the one hand, and machine-made, standardized, and industrial processes on the other. It suggests the difference between a home-cooked burger, with spices added that come to hand, and the decision to use a frying pan, indoor grill, or outdoor grill made based on taste preferences, convenience, or other contingencies, versus a McDonald's Big Mac, which has been designed to have no variability wherever and whenever and by whomever it is made (since workers need to be replaceable), the ultimate fantasy of American industrial food. Or at the high end of this same trend to control lies molecular gastronomy and all kinds of augmented and virtual experiences promising the taste of sushi or birthday cake without the mess of human hands—cooking or eating—just grab your headset and aromatic diffusers, and dive in.[1] Pye recognizes the speed and scale offered by the workmanship of certainty and thus does not simply argue for the superiority of risk. But he argues that creativity in design can only come through risk. In a sense, then, Sahlins is not irrelevant to this discussion either as in the top-down attempt to remove variability from the process of cooking, there is, perhaps potentially no longer a risk of categories in practice.

Another way that Pye frames the distinction between risk and certainty is in discussing skill. Skill means there is variability, possibility of control and different outcomes. The opposite of this is "determining systems" (1969: 54). Skilled systems allow for the possibility of changing course midstream, and indeed, he suggests that this allows the possibility of learning from errors, as well as a kind of making that draws on unexpected memories and analogies. Once again, he bemoans the crowding out of skilled systems by determining systems. Writing in the 1960s, Pye notes:

> There is now a widespread aversion from skill. In making we try, if we can, to eliminate skill by using know-how and determining systems. In music and sport we prefer that few should have skill while many listen or watch . . . The word "foolproof" in an advertisement is taken as an inducement [think cake mix]. By using one word for skill and know-how we effectively conceal this aversion from ourselves. (1969: 56)

Pye's contrast, then, touches on larger questions and attitudes toward meaning and value under contemporary capitalism, and questions that go back to Marx, Ruskin, and Morris about whether technology, the marketplace, and/or corporate capitalism are essentially alienating to human experience. Does craft, or DIY, constitute a resistance or a handmaid to capitalism? And what is "craft" anyway? These are broad questions that I cannot hope to give satisfactory answers to here. However, they will all be touched on in thinking through the implications of an approach to cooking that sees everyday risk as part of our embodied and intimate relationship to ingredients, processes, and a cooking/kitchen environment. Anthropologically, speaking, this chapter will take the work of Tim Ingold as muse, and suggest some of the ways that Ingold's approach might complement Sahlins's while also questioning a number of aspects of Ingold's approach.

DEFINITIONS OF CRAFT

The approach I take here positions cooking as a type of craft practice. But what is craft? Just as anthropologists have argued that "modernity" is an empty signifier, which can take on different meanings "wherever it lands" (Comaroff and Comaroff 1993), craft, as a term often used in opposition to modernity as "traditional" practice,[2] has also been claimed to be an empty signifier which "marks—perhaps it also tries to hide—cultural ruptures" (DeNicola and Wilkinson-Weber 2016: 5). Alicia DeNicola and Clare Wilkinson-Weber usefully criticize "craft nostalgia" and the idea that craft as small-scale "plucky survival" against the most alienating aspects of modern life must be balanced against the hybridity of all forms of production, which includes elements of mechanization and of "handmade." So in this regard the same critiques that anthropologists and historians have leveled at notions of "tradition" and "authenticity" would apply to craft as well. At a time when "craft beer" is marketed by Budweiser and "handmade" could be applied to iPhones made in Chinese factories,[3] such concerns about "craft" as a particular content seem well warranted.

A different approach would focus on craft as a form of making, rather than a content, and puts us more in line with Pye's ideas discussed above. Such a view can be derived from Richard Sennett's philosophical tome *The Craftsman*, as well as anthropologists like Lucy Suchman working on the alternative sensory embodiments of paper and pencil and computer-aided design (CAD) for engineers or Mike Press exploring the workmanship of risk in "digital crafting."[4] Sennett also argues for a more inclusive conception of craft that includes "ancient weavers and Linux programmers" (2008: 21) and focuses on processes of learning through repetition,[5] engagement with materials and with other humans, and the use of the hand as well as the head.

"The Craftsman represents the special human condition of being *engaged*" (2008: 20; emphasis in original).[6]

Food anthropologist Amy Trubek builds a picture of cooking as craft that resonates with such process-focused approaches. As she notes, one possible definition of craft in cooking is "the reproduction of a shared culinary repertoire" that implies a particular social and sensory context. Indeed, she draws on my ethnographic work on Kalymnos to describe such a tradition-based view. She suggests a second view that sees craft as "skillful-based practice" (2017: 156). Such skillful practice requires a certain kind of engagement, like Sennett, it involves tacit knowledge and "evidence of the hand," though not necessarily "from scratch" (2017: 186). Thus, her view of craft is one that fits very well with Pye's contrast between risk and certainty. Her key example is the work of artisan bakers such as Gerard Rubaud and Chad Robertson, who work with wild yeast and other natural fermentation processes that can be guided but not controlled in the sense of producing the same product each time. Bakers work between a state of "control" and "chaos," relying on "a set of principles as to kneading, shaping and baking the bread" and managing processes that rely on intuition and are very difficult to scale into the consistency of industrial products (Trubek 2017: 177–79). This bread baking is, then, responsive to the changing material and social environment in which it takes place. Similarly, in her ethnography of Vermont cheese makers, Heather Paxson (2013) cites Pye's idea of risk and lack of predetermined outcome as an essential aspect of what makes cheese making "artisanal."

What makes these practices "crafty" is, then, a type of engagement with the material and social worlds of making that have not been standardized and directed from above through capitalist management practices by administrative fiat, or the overly elaborated jigs of assembly line production that Pye would put at the "certainty" end of the scale. Craft involves a submission to the contingencies of *The World beyond Your Head* (2015) to take the title of Matthew Crawford's book. In it he argues that a long philosophical tradition on human autonomy has combined with the technological magic of contemporary culture to create a situation in which most of our experience is "distracted" from the kind of development of skill and craft being described here. It is only by attentively re-engaging with the material world and with other people that we can have direct, unmediated experiences which will "put [ourselves] at risk" (2015: 187), here posing craft as much as a social identity as it is a material practice.

Jeweler Bruce Metcalf develops similar thoughts on what he calls the "Myth of Modernism" (2007) in which he specifically poses craft in relation to the "contingencies" that artistic modernism has dispatched. Metcalf argues that craft has long suffered under the shadow of a modernist ideology developed in twentieth-century art practice, which drew from Kant to argue for the value of aesthetics that are autonomous, detached, and disinterested from all of the "contingencies" of content and context. Craft that embraced modernist ideals rejected meaning, tradition, politics, usefulness, even skill, in pursuit of abstract form (Metcalf 2007: 12–13). He notes that a bowl used for oatmeal could not be "art" in this understanding of aesthetics, and that "you would have to stop using it as a bowl before you could perceive it aesthetically" (10). The same would no doubt be the case for the taste of food itself.

Metcalf suggests that modernist art was the "high" version of manufacture, thus craft was squeezed out at one end by factory production—in people's ordinary consumption practices—and at the other by modernist art. What was left out of this understanding were, in fact, what Metcalf calls the "contingencies" of society and everyday life that gave meaning and value to particular objects. Metcalf suggests that the appropriate response to this is to reconnect with the "craftness" of craft,[7] by embracing the value of contingency, which includes a connection to tradition, usefulness, meaning, and politics (craft is, for Metcalf, a critique of factory production as well). As he sums up, "My thesis is that craft is inherently a contingent artform, and its aesthetic value must be located in the ways craft is intimate, useful and meaningful" (18). Metcalf's approach to craft certainly resonates with Pye's "workmanship of risk," although by substituting contingency for risk Metcalf suggests a broadened applicability, and why craft might not just oppose the workmanship of certainty, but as with Crawford, would oppose the focus on detachment and autonomy in Western modernity. I would, however, draw out Metcalf's use of contingency to suggest a broader sense of engagement not just with tradition, usefulness, and the political, but also (and this is implied in his work, I think) the recalcitrance and possibilities of engagement with the material world.

TIM INGOLD: CRAFT AS SKILL

Re-engaging with the material world and criticizing the abstractions of modernity is very much part of the project of anthropologist Tim Ingold whose work focuses particularly on processes of "making" through his analysis of skill and "enskilment." In particular, he wants to avoid the idealism of modernity that wants to impose abstract forms onto a willing and plastic world around us.

While Ingold does not focus on cooking, he often seems drawn to cooking-based metaphors in his work. In his book *Making* (2013), he imagines in his introduction a thought-experiment: an elfin trickster has switched the places of a Scottish cookbook and Pierre Bourdieu's *Outline of a Theory of Practice* on your bookshelf. You hungrily go into the kitchen to make Scottish herrings in oatmeal and find instead some indecipherable prose about *habitus*. Returning frustrated to your office to finish your article for the journal *Anthropologica Theoretica* you find, instead of that perfect quote, instructions on cleaning herring. Ingold poses his own book as "clos[ing] the gap" (2013: 14–15) between the abstractions of scholarship and the practicalities of cooking as his own metaphor more broadly for processes of making and living in the world and how they have been attenuated by Western thought and contemporary society.

Ingold has long been interested in upsetting traditional Western dichotomies such as nature–culture and human–non-human. In *Making,* he hones in on the dichotomy of matter and form in arguing against traditional notions of "design" as a kind of pre-shaping of material that determines its outcome. He criticizes a "hylomorphic" approach that sees making as a process of imposing ideas onto objects. In contrast, he proposes a "morphogenetic" process in which the maker adds his own energies to the forces and materials already in play in the world (2013: 21). As he puts it:

> To read making longitudinally, as a confluence of forces and materials, rather than laterally as a transposition from image to object, is to regard it as such a form-generating—or *morphogenetic*—process. . . . This is not of course to deny that the maker may have an idea in mind of what he wants to make . . . Suffice it to say, at this point, that even if the maker has a form in mind, it is not this form that creates the work. It is the engagement with materials. (2013: 22)

In a chapter called "The Sighted Watchmaker," Ingold takes on the notion of the "Blind Watchmaker" associated with Richard Dawkins's particular evolutionist attack on creationism. In analyzing the debate, Ingold shows the shared presuppositions of both sides, based on the hylomorphic worldview, that "there can be no functional complexity without prior design" (2013: 67). Such an approach "asks only how the watch was designed but has nothing to say about how it might have been put together, or about the craftsmanship and dexterity involved in doing so" (2013: 66). When talking not metaphorically about watches, but rather about living creatures, Dawkins applies the same logic: "once you have a design for a bat, you effectively have a bat" (2013: 66). He argues, in effect, that evolutionary theorists like Dawkins are constantly engaged in a circular reasoning by which they model the observed behavior of living organisms and then project that model onto the design of the creature—the DNA—which is then held responsible for all observable outcomes.

Ingold's response to this approach is to delve further into the metaphor of the watchmaker, engaging with craft and apprenticeship theory and drawing on Richard Sennett among others to argue that the role of the craftsperson (here watch designer) is not to prespecify results, but to "see forward" to anticipate and to be "'one step ahead of the material'" (Sennett cited in Ingold 2013: 69). The craftsperson works "*in and among* the pieces, rather than *above and beyond* them" (2013: 69, emphasis in original). Rather than the architect, making plans to be executed, he suggests once again an image of a cook (or gardener) employing "imaginative foresight" (2013: 72)—perhaps "foresmell" and "foretaste" would be more appropriate here?—in order to bring materials into "correspondence" (2013: 70). Indeed, he suggests that both in creative design and in our everyday moving through the world, illustrated by Ingold in "setting the table" for breakfast, we are constantly caught between imaginative foresight and the "drag of material abrasion" (2013: 72) and this dichotomy, rather than one between abstract planning and material execution, is central to the processes of "making."[8]

It is in these notions of the craftsman's relationship with contingent and possibly recalcitrant materials that we see how Ingold's approach overlaps with Pye's notion of the workmanship of risk. The workmanship of certainty is certainly described by the hylomorphic imposition of previously established form onto matter, where ideally, as Sahlins would say, there is no "risk of categories in practice" because everything turns out exactly as planned. By contrast, Ingold uses the concept of "workmanship of risk" in describing the process of working with tools such as a hand-held saw to cut wood: "when working with a saw, as with any other hand-held tool, the result is never a foregone conclusion; rather there is an ever-present danger, throughout the work, that it may go awry" (2011: 59). Ingold sees this risk both as part of the engagement of working with materials as well as something that the craftsman may act to mitigate in various ways by using jigs and templates to increase reliability at certain moments in the process. He also notes that there is always the possibility of risk "creep[ing] into the most apparently predetermined of operations" (Ingold 2011: 59), thus requiring continuous attention from the craftsman. Even if, as with Pye, Ingold sees risk and certainty as on a continuum, he wishes to distinguish the craftsman from the machine operative: "a workman of certainty, whose activity is constrained by the parameters of a determining system." For the workman of certainty, "the intimate coupling between movement and perception that governs the work of the craftsman is broken" (2011: 59). Ingold argues that in the development of skill through repetition the craftsman develops a growing awareness, rather than losing awareness, to habitual action. It is what Ingold calls the "rhythmic pulse of dexterous activity" that guides the workmanship of risk, so that every cut of the sawblade (or the kitchen knife) is both similar and different and must be constantly adjusted to contingent circumstances. This contrasts, once again, with the loss of attention created by attempts to impose a workmanship of certainty not through the craftsman's jig, but through the "metronomic oscillations of mechanically determining systems" (2013: 61), a metaphor meant to suggest the transfer of skills from humans and tools to the technological world of automaticity and algorithms, the dream of capitalism and modernity. But Ingold hedges this critique by suggesting, albeit briefly,[9] that those machines are not in themselves impervious to their own imperfections and perturbations in the environment, so that they too require the kind of skill of the craftsman: "Thus skill is destined to carry on for as long as life does, along a line of resistance, forever undoing the closures and finalities that mechanization throws in its path" (2013: 62). For Ingold, we continue to engage, or at least potentially engage, with machines in ways that allow for us to avoid becoming Marx's "living appendages of lifeless mechanism." Machines can, of course, explicitly call for intimacy and attention even when they do not work as Ingold's classic tools. Faced with my Behmor 1600 AB Plus coffee roaster ("with patented smoke suppressing technology"), I note that the instruction manual repeats four separate times that the Behmor "is not a set and walk away device," but is meant to be monitored during the entirety of its operation. Further, I am told to roast the smallest batch of coffee (1/4 lb.) on the basic setting for the first four times I use it, so that I develop an understanding of "the subtle nuances . . . including the snapping sounds and aromas associated with a completed roast," since coffee roasting "is not simply done by pushing buttons on a piece of equipment. It is an interactive process that relies heavily on the senses and decisions of the user." Even before I am enjoined to start roasting, I read numerous tips on the sensory properties to look for—Ingold's "foresight"—such as not expecting the appearance of oiliness of beans as a sign of doneness, and "Always forward think your roast by fifteen seconds." Indeed, with machines like the Behmor, one might certainly be reassured by the "law of the conservation of skills" (Ingold 2013: 62). Bruno Latour has referred to fears about machines taking away our souls more forcefully, describing the fantasy that "the uprooted, acculturated, Americanized, scientified, technologized Westerner [has become] a Spock-like mutant.[10] Have we not shed enough tears over the disenchantment of the world?" (Latour 1993: 115). For Latour, as opposed to Crawford and to some extent Ingold, everything and every time period is full of hybrids of humans and technology, and fears of the loss of skill are simply modernist fantasies.

TWO PARADIGMS OF RISK: INGOLD AND SAHLINS

This might be a good moment to compare Ingold's understanding of risk with Sahlins's and how it might help us make sense of cooking through the role of recipes. Recipes are another avatar of the literate and the modern that are easy to oppose to the authentic cooking of ordinary folk (see, e.g., Giard 1998). And indeed, recipes that call for careful measurements, and the exactitude implied, do partake of an ideology of separating cooking from the skilled, embodied human cook.[11] Ingold is certainly critical of the metaphor of recipes in understanding practice, as suggested above. Ingold explicitly criticizes the notion developed by cognitive anthropologist Dan Sperber that culture can be seen as transmitted in ways similar to how a recipe for mornay sauce could be transmitted and then simply "convert[ed] into bodily behavior" (Sperber cited in Ingold 2001: 137). Ingold, like other scholars thinking about cooking,[12] points out all of the tacit knowledge that goes into cooking and that could not be captured in the pre-existing form of a written recipe. He suggests this through describing his own teaching of his daughter how to get the feel for cracking an egg, something that can only be under-stood, he suggests, through one's engagement with the process: "Evidently in cookery, as much as in any other field of practical activity, people do not acquire their knowledge ready-made but rather *grow into* it, through a pro-cess that might be called *guided rediscovery*" (Ingold 2011: 305–6; empha-sis in original). Ingold avoids the old anthropological term "enculturation" here, but I think it is also appropriate to think about what he is describing.

In my earlier work on memory, I argued, based on my Greek ethnogra-phy, explicitly against the idea that cooking is learned through written reci-pes (Sutton 2001: chap. 5). This was part of a first approach to questions of memory and the "transmission of knowledge," which my Greek informants insisted occurred through firsthand, oral communication: "It passes from mother to daughter." More recently (Sutton 2014), I also refined this tru-ism—from mother to daughter—to suggest a much more complex process of conflict not captured through any straightforward appeal to tradition or transmission. The "it" of transmission, of course, was much more than a se-ries of recipes, but rather what Ingold calls a "taskscape," a set of bodily and sensory orientations that are developed through participation in social life. It is because of such taskscapes that everyone's experience in the kitchen is different and worth ethnographic analysis. Or as Giard puts it in arguing for a focus on particularized "tactics" in the kitchen, even if two people are care-fully following the same recipe, experienced cooks will create something different "[b]ecause other elements intervene in the preparation: a personal touch, the knowledge or ignorance of tiny secret practices . . . an entire *rela-tionship to things* that the recipe does not codify and hardly clarifies" (1998: 201, emphasis in original). This relationship to things is very much what is at stake when one thinks about skill and the workmanship of risk.

And yet, recipes do play a role in cooking. As much as Ingold describes processes of learning with acuity, his analysis does not seem to capture the importance people also place on recipes as knowledge, whether written[13] or oral. This knowledge may be fully developed as free-standing recipes for specific dishes or broken down into smaller units, the "tricks" that Kalymnians would share (or not share) with each other about how to deal with certain contingencies, to make the most of new or old ingredients, or to produce familiar and unfamiliar flavors. Here I found the insights of Charles Keller and Janet Keller (1999) on blacksmithing more helpful, and more in line with Sahlins's approach, in that they focus attention both on those moments of skill analyzed by Ingold as well as the "stock of knowledge" of goals, outcomes, and various ways of attaining them that the blacksmith builds up over the course of becoming a skilled practitioner. There is also a stock of knowledge of appropriate and desired tastes, much discussed on Kalymnos, that form part of a sensory regime (Howes 2003) that emphasizes taste and smell as key ways of creating proper food and proper social lives; I explore this elsewhere under the label of "gustemology." Indeed, sensory outcomes—what foods taste good in what combinations and undergoing what processes—is discussed on a daily basis not just by practitioners but by those who may have little direct experience in the kitchen, making up part of the sensory scape of the Kalymnian stock of knowledge. Ingold does not deny that something like a "stock of knowledge" might exist for the skilled practitioner, though he does analytically downplay it in his desire to focus on emergent properties of any encounter. In the same chapter on tool use he writes of "the alignment of present circumstances to the conjunctions of the past . . . Every use of a tool, in short, is a remembering of how to use it, which at once picks up the strands of past practice and carries them forward in current contexts" (2013: 57). These strands of past practice may not be quite the same as Sahlins's categories, but I would suggest that some degree of flexible, embodied, but still categorical and to some limited extent abstractable knowledge ("tricks") is at play.[14] Beyond that, how might we think about the role of recipes as named dishes, and what might they tell us about cooking as process?

Whether or not people think of cooking as "creative" or as mundane drudgery, people generally do set out to make something, a cooked meal does not emerge from a simple engagement with ingredients, indeed people often have a very strong sense of what they are intending to make when cooking. As many of my Kalymnian cooking subjects would tell me, they often decided on what they would make for their main meal the night before, sometimes because they had a desire for a dish that they had not had for a period of time. And on Kalymnos this process is further aided by the regularities of the seasonal and religious calendar by which Wednesdays and Fridays are typically bean dishes—white beans, lentils, occasionally chickpeas or fava beans, Saturday often a lighter meal, and Sunday a special meal such as moussaka or stuffed grape leaves. On Kalymnos naming these dishes was not simply naming an ingredient—say, fava beans—but also a whole raft of associated knowledge of how fava beans should be prepared, what other ingredients were necessary (e.g., tomatoes), optional (parsley), and unacceptable (carrots), and questions about the type of water to soak the beans in (rain water versus spring water) the previous night. These are what I would argue for analytical purposes are the "structures," or stock of knowledge of cooking: knowledge of ingredients, techniques, and tools, rhythms associated with planning (soaking beans the night before, procuring the proper soaking water), as well as all of the aspects of the flavors, textures, visual cues, and other outcomes that people use to assess a dish as they are eating it. Sometimes this knowledge can be very explicitly transferred, as when a grandmother explains to her granddaughter that if you know how to make white beans you can also make chickpeas or fava beans, though with fava beans, you might want to discard the first water after boiling to get rid of the bitterness, and with chickpeas you might want to add orzo (*manestra*).[15] These are tips that are taught not at the moment of cooking, but as part of a more general stock of knowledge that a young woman might be expected to slowly develop on Kalymnos. I also note that YouTube star Helen Rennie, founder of Helen's Kitchen Cooking School in Boston, suggests developing a similar stock of knowledge for the purposes of improvisation through thinking about the ingredients in each dish that you eat, abstracting them to general categories, and imagining recombining them in dishes that you make. She says that when she sets out to make a kale salad she "simply thinks of all the kale salad's I've ever eaten . . . when I'm eating out it can be a little miserable because everything I put in my mouth becomes instantly compared to all the previous versions of this dish."[16] She compares it to having a memory chip in her brain, but only for food. I will return to this issue in my discussion of memory as a sense in the next chapter, but for now I simply note that whether one has prodigious memory powers or not, some mental process of this kind that allows us to imagine certain structures in our minds is part of the cooking process.

Cooking is, following Ingold, indeed not simply the execution of these structures. As I have argued elsewhere, for example, Kalymnians are constantly adjusting their cooking techniques to the contingencies of their sociomaterial environment in which ingredients may be of varying quality, social pressures and daily life may intervene in familiar cooking processes, and the desires and dislikes of those who will be eating may influence cooking practices, as well as claims and associations of particular techniques or ingredients with varying identities or levels of identity ("traditional," "modern," "local," "cosmopolitan," etc.). These structures do, however, play a role as people plan, adjust, and assess their cooking work both while cooking, and while eating the cooked dish.[17] And this is not just a facet of Kalymnian cooking. As renowned chef Jacques Pepin argues, challenging the hegemonic view in the United States of the recipe as blueprint,[18] "The recipe is only the expression of one moment in time, the day that I did it, in fact, when I did the recipe before it probably was different than it is now."[19] This comes just after Pepin has discussed a small adjustment to soften his Brussel sprouts cooking in a pan by adding a little bit of water as one of the "tricks of the trade." Tricks of the trade, then, are very much in line with Ingold's critique of the blueprint; they are the hack that allows you to produce a flavorful dish not as pure execution of a plan, but as a negotiation with contingency. And yet, Pepin would not deny that there are structures (tastes, recipes, etc.) that guide us. Here, then, in talking about a pan of Brussel sprouts, Pepin captures both Sahlins's understanding that the reproduction of a structure always entails its transformation at the same time he expresses ideas about the skill involved in cooking that would be familiar to Ingold.

Pepin's insight is key to how I would propose to see everyday cooking. Each time, literally each day that one cooks, one sets out to make something, though of course, as noted, in particular sociomaterial circumstances and constraints. In doing so, in making an X, that category X is put at risk as a multitude of contingencies, material resistances, and potential improvisations come into play in determining the eventual outcome of the dish.[20] While on a typical day these may not be particularly noticeable, they also have the potential to stretch the category since something that looks or tastes slightly different is eaten under the same label. This is what Sahlins refers to as the "great gamble with empirical realities" as the label insists on continuity, while practice will always produce some change.

To reduce the contingencies, and thereby the possibilities, once again is the goal of the "workmanship of certainty," where removing or limiting skill in the service of replicability is often the point. But it makes for an impoverished type of cooking, one that seems to stress all of the problematic aspects of modernity, in Crawford's terms, autonomy and disassociation from the world of material contingencies, in Ingold's a loss of the intimacy and engagement that is a fundamental part of his view of humanity as a creature "dwelling" in a shifting environment.

CONTEMPORARY COOKING TRENDS
AND CULINARY PERFECTIONISM

Craft is a useful framework for thinking about cooking as everyday risk specifically because it highlights some key oppositions in contemporary cooking trends. As with other aspects of our current world, Ingold's point is to suggest that there is an ongoing struggle between contextually situated knowledge and the creation of algorithms of practice (Ingold 2011: 61) that allow for the reduction of the "risk" that is part and parcel of human engagement with the world. Or, as James Carrier (2012: 703) puts it: "[There is] a general desire to replace individual skill, experience, and knowledge of context in decision-making with procedures that are seen as impersonal and objective, the 'best practice' of modern management-speak."[21] This is also what culture critic Evgeny Morozov dubs "technological solutionism," or "recasting all complex social situations either as neatly defined problems with definite, computable solutions or as transparent and self-evident processes that can be easily optimized" (2013: 5).[22]

I have applied this approach to practices of cooking in Greece, arguing that seemingly inefficient choices such as the prevalent technique of cutting ingredients—from onions and potatoes to eggplant to loaves of bread—in the hand, rather than setting them down on a counter, must be interpreted against a larger social and sensory taskscape. In other words, a context in which they make sense as part of Greek cooking in which the cook does not turn her body away from wider interactions but remains engaged in the social scene. Cooking skills are exercised, reproduced and changed in a context in which Kalymnians observe their own and others' practices, share and hide secrets, praise and criticize procedures and results, and carefully taste, compare, and remember what Kalymnian food should taste like. Elsewhere, I compared Kalymnian cutting of vegetables to this description from Ingold of the skilled sawing of a piece of wood: "Although a confident, regular movement ensures an even cut, no two strokes are ever precisely the same. With each stroke I have to adjust my posture ever so slightly to allow for the advancing groove, and for possible irregularities in the grain of the wood" (Ingold 2011: 52). He summarizes: "Cutting wood . . . is an effect not of the saw alone but of the entire system of forces and relations set up by the intimate engagement of the saw, the trestle, the workpiece and my own body" (Ingold 2011: 56). In the same way, cutting Kalymnian-style effectively replaces the solid balance of a cutting surface with the intimacy and control of the hand/object. Each cut is felt—not just by the hand that is holding the knife, but by the hand that holds the object to be cut—and allows for adjustments to be made as the hand rotates the object. There are local standards for Kalymnian cutting and Kalymnian cooking more generally. But they are not of the form that holds that there is an ideal, rationalized, and efficient way of doing things, the kind of culinary perfectionism or Taylorism that often seems to pervade US popular culture. For example, a regular cooking feature on the artsy liberal blog *Slate* is titled "You're Doing It Wrong." Here, readers can learn about how they are preparing pasta, cornbread, pancakes, and many other things "wrong." Imagine my surprise when I read the headline "The Undisputed Right Way to Chop an Onion."[23] Nodding to a lack of pretention, the author/blogger states that she will "show you the right way to chop an onion according to chefs and experts everywhere." She further goes on to note (in text accompanying a video) that "[p]erhaps onions' ubiquity is the reason pretty much everyone agrees on the right way to chop them. As a species, humans have had enough experience with onions to agree." Unsurprisingly, all of Greece would, under this definition, be "doing it wrong." What is striking on a website that is otherwise careful to take multi-culturalism seriously is that there remains a mundane everyday assumption that cooking techniques are simply beyond the realm of interpretation. In Kalymnos, there is right and wrong but in a very different sense.

More than right and wrong, at least the blogger still wishes we engage with cooking as a hands-on activity. Many other current trends, both "high" and "low" would dispense with the messiness, the chore, the engagement with cooking. On the "low" or mundane end, no doubt, the pasta company Barilla introduced a pasta in the mid-2010s that allows you to save the trouble of boiling water in advance, cooking pasta as if it were rice, whatever the gooey results, a kind of disembedding of the cook from the arduous process of checking your pasta for doneness, whether tasted, thrown against the wall, or broken in half to reveal the uncooked dot.

At the middling to high end there is, for example, sous vide cooking, in which "you have none of the normal sensory cues that a meal is cooking: the smell of garlic sizzling in oil, the *blip-blip* of risotto in a pot . . . You set the water bath to the required temperature, vacuum seal the food in the bag, submerge the bags, set the timer, and wait for the bleep. No stirring, no basting, no prodding or tasting. No human input at all" (Wilson 2012: 253–54).[24] Sous vide cooking has come in for increasing criticism as professional chefs note that it is a way to "circumvent the annoying business of actually cooking food . . . by the traditional methods of touch, feel and timing,"[25] useful perhaps in certain restaurant contexts where consistency is important, but for ordinary cooks the opposite of cooking with skill.

And then there are the designs for "smart" kitchens that will observe the cook's movements and inform them "whenever they have deviated from their chosen recipe" (Morozov 2013: 11). In the name of efficiency, the very joys of cooking represented by a sense of mastery are sacrificed for the presumed improvement in taste (Sutton 2014: 194). A less dictatorial version of this is the idea that the majority of "millennials" now cook with videos playing on their iPhone or tablets in the background. While this may seem like a contemporary version of the long reliance on written recipes and recipe advice in the United States, some researchers suggest that this leads to "cognitive offloading" so that the kind of skills of improvisation discussed in this chapter do not flourish.[26]

Meanwhile, AI (artificial intelligence) is increasingly suggested to play a greater role in cooking. The IBM supercomputer named Watson is using its database of flavor compounds to come up with new ingredient pairings that generic humans will like. Strawberries with mushrooms are apparently high on its list of suggestions.[27] And the company Moley Robotics has been promising consumers, after a number of delays, "the world's first fully-automated and integrated intelligent cooking robot," based on AI and motion-capture technology, and with access to the dishes of some of the world's leading celebrity chefs, and ability to set calorie counts and incorporate any dietary restrictions of its user.[28] An article on the cooking robot, which was estimated in 2017 to retail for $92,000, contains some interesting responses from some of the chefs whose skill the robot is aiming to capture. Executive chef Austin Gresham notes:

> Professional chefs have to improvise constantly as they prepare dishes. If a recipe says to bake a potato for 25 minutes and the potatoes are more or less dense than the previous batch, then cooking times will vary. I would challenge any machine to make as good a mashed potato (from scratch) as a cook who works for Joel Robuchon. Additionally, pots, pans, ovens, and grills have hot and cold spots. A chef has to quickly improvise and turn sheet pans in ovens, not use certain spots on a grill and certain pans etc.[29]

Notably the key issue for Greshem is contingency, or the particularity of ingredients, tools, and circumstances that require the constant adjustments to the environment discussed above. The author notes as much in suggesting that human sensory input is a key part of the cooking process: the sense of touch allows one to understand where one is in the process of kneading dough, for example (see Sutton 2014: 54–56). Executive chef Virgile Brandel stresses a more generalized "human touch" in contemplating the robot. "Chefs put a little bit of themselves into every meal that is prepared, making no two dishes identical."[30] This sense of each iteration of a dish as different and non-identical gets very much to the notion of the workmanship of risk versus certainty. While, as I noted, this is always something of a continuum, and at some, perhaps undetectable level, two McDonald's Big Macs are non-identical, the extent to which difference and "risk" is removed is often the extent to which people distinguish "cooking" from "non-cooking." In 2012, during my research on Kalymnos, I showed a video of the "mombot," an earlier Japanese iteration of the cooking robot restricted to making omelets and miso soup, to my friend Dimitris Roditis. I was interested in his reaction to it because he was a computer programmer and technophile who had basically single-handedly introduced most of the computers to Kalymnos in the 1990s. Despite his "modernizing" tendencies, Dimitris was horrified by the prospect of eating the product of a mombot. He told me he found

the idea of robot cooks deeply disturbing, commenting that a dish is simply not supposed to be the same each time.[31] Or as my colleague, Leonidas
Vournelis, put it: "If you reproduce a dish that is the same as the recipe you
used, what have I learned about you? Nothing!"

How different this was from the attitude expressed in American culture's
fascination with the "perfect recipe." Just as with the notion of the "perfect
way" to cut an onion, perfect recipes create a notion of reproduction that
is at odds with the reality of the shifting contingencies of cooking. As John
Finn notes: "perfect recipes do more than make bad cooks—they make bad
citizens because they encourage habits of docility and deference, both of
which are inimical to democratic citizenship" (2011: 503). This also raises
the issue, noted by Finn, that such expertise is often gendered male, and
those presumed in need of advice are often female, adding to the power dynamics of the notion of perfection promulgated here. Despite the significant
changes in gender roles in the past fifty years in US society, it is still likely to
be women who are at risk of being judged lesser for failing to attain the standards of perfection promoted in this way, a different kind of risk than that of
Pye's workmanship of risk for sure, in which the policing (and self-policing)
of traditional gender identities is at stake.

Finn notes in his discussion that part of the appeal of the perfect recipe
in the United States may be the sense that many people feel that they do not
have a "stock of accumulated praxis to draw upon, no reserve of cultural or
embodied familial wisdom" (2011: 506). Nevertheless, he argues that even
if voluntarily submitted to, there is a potential for "tyranny" in the submission to the power and control of the perfect recipe that extends, in Finn's
view, well beyond the kitchen.[32] He singles out Christopher Kimball's *Cook's
Illustrated* and his kitchen—featured in the show *America's Test Kitchen*—as
key purveyors of notions of the perfect. He argues, for example, that one
category of the perfect is the notion of "perfection as repetition" in which
the idea that recipes are tried in the test kitchen up to fifty times to make
sure that the results are "foolproof."[33] Finn also shows that *Cooks Illustrated*
develops the idea of perfect in technique, in other words particular rules that
can be followed that promise the same results even with "little culinary skill"
(2011: 507).

We see here the influence of the workmanship of certainty and the promise of replicability it provides. In this world, there is no risk at play, and
no emergent properties of situations or new discoveries. Presumably one
missing ingredient or a malfunctioning tool would be enough to destroy the
entire edifice. Furthermore, Finn notes, though does not discuss at length,
the fact that perfection is here defined in a Platonic sense: "Some forms are
inferior, some are superior, but only one is *perfect*" (2011: 507, emphasis in
original). This is very different from the Kalymnian sense of evaluation, in

which good taste and good recipes are always defined in relation to particular (often shared) standards, goals, and values.

I have followed Christopher Kimball's work since the early 2010s, when I first noticed the kind of oppositions that Finn points to in discussing *Cooks Illustrated*. Since then Kimball's ventures include a new magazine and podcast called *Milk Street*. Perhaps responsive to some of the critiques leveled against him, Kimball strikes a milder tone in *Milk Street*, not as insistent, in my reading, on notions of the perfect, more willing to embrace fallibility—his own and that of others—as part of the cooking process. Ideas about the nature of cooking as normalized and rule-governed, however, do still come out in interesting ways. I was struck, for example, by a discussion between Kimball and cookbook author Melissa Clark, which I quote below to illustrate the relevance of an Ingoldian approach to thinking of cooking as a skilled, emergent practice rather than an application of abstract rules. Clark says that her cookbook *Dinner: Changing the Game* (2017) is a critique of the lingering 1950s paradigm of mothers and grandmothers in the kitchen creating recognizable dinners of meat and two sides. She suggests instead many different paths to contemporary "dinner," explicitly critiquing notions of perfection: "a path out of the tyranny of a perfectly composed plate with three distinct elements in separate little piles. The chicken, the carrots, the rice. The meatloaf, the mashed potatoes, the peas" (2017: 13). Interesting that such structured meals recalling Mary Douglas's A + 2b might still be taken as the image of perfection in our contemporary times (just as the lingering assumptions about gendered responsibility in the kitchen that I noted above). Kimball would no doubt agree, with his offerings always featuring many multicultural possibilities. However, in his interview with Clark, after assenting to this general idea, he challenges her claim that "there are very few hard and fast rules when it comes to cooking." The subsequent discussion is as follows:

CHRISTOPHER KIMBALL: I don't know whether I totally agree with that or totally disagree with that. I wonder whether . . . there actually are rules when you spend a lot of time in the kitchen like if you spend a lot of time being a musician you sort of—the rules become part of you, so you don't think of them as rules. And so then you can just go do stuff. But you really know there are rules. And so aren't there really a lot of rules when it comes to cooking. Aren't there a lot of things you just shouldn't do? Or you think at this point, you know, you can break all the rules and be a good cook?

MELISSA CLARK: I also used to think when you go into a kitchen (chefs) there are rules, there is this gold standard technique that you need to learn, and I was obsessed with getting the technique right, and as I worked with different chefs I realized that there is no one technique. There are so many different techniques. You go into Daniel Belou's kitchen and he cuts an onion differently than the Bromberg brothers. And neither was right nor wrong, but they give slightly different flavors to the end dish. So I think that the rules are yeah, don't burn the house down and don't cut your finger off, but aside from that I think there's a lot of leeway. And there's also what you need to do as a cook at a more advanced level is understand what you want in the dish and learn how you get there by learning different techniques, but I really don't believe in one technique that all chefs need to learn. And that's very freeing for the home cook too because you know what, if you're doing it your way and it tastes good, you just keep doing it your way, and that's working out just fine, because I don't think people should feel inadequate because they haven't internalized all these professional techniques.

CK (changes topic): Let's talk about roasting a chicken.[34]

A number of things are notable here. Kimball accepts that cooking "rules" can be tacit, incorporated into the body just like the rules of music for a jazz musician, or as Connerton suggests, a "memory in the hands" (1989: 93). But for Kimball these are still rules, to suggest less would be, no doubt, to invite chaos. I believe this is still in line with Ingold's notion of the hylomorphic worldview, in which, to repeat: "there can be no functional complexity without prior design" (2013: 67). The design, here, is on the level of shared, agreed upon, "perfect" techniques and procedures that must be mastered before embarking on cooking a dish—the "perfect" way to slice an onion, for example. Clark, by contrast, suggests that what rules there are, are not Finn's "perfect technique" but rather the rules of thumb—like do not cut off your thumb—that Ingold sees as part of the enskillment and education of attention that he argues are part of a non-modernist, morphogenetic approach to creating forms. To reiterate, this refers to the emergent, risky practice of being responsive to the myriad uncertainties of ingredients, tools, and the larger cooking environment. This can be freeing for the cook, as both Finn and Clark note, by not holding them to some pre-determined standard of perfection and often reinforcing traditional feminine gender roles in the process (Finn 2011: 512).

An interesting discussion of recipe writing with another alumna of *America's Test Kitchen* Rachel Greenhouse, raises similar issues when addressing the question of how to write a recipe. She has the job of translating recipes written by trained chefs into something readable by a general public who, it is assumed, has little of the tacit knowledge of cooking that many recipes assume. Greenhouse frames this as follows: "If someone's only going to read what's on this page, will they be able to make this dish exactly like they need to in order to succeed."[35] She notes all the assumptions that go into this process, including basics like "that you have a stove, that you have refrigeration, that you know what tool to use when I say stir." Greenhouse interestingly contrasts her role with that of a food blogger who is free to use all kinds of subjective words like "delectable, nummy," whereas "I would never use those words because we're trying to come from a more objective point of view, and the words we tend to use are perfect, or foolproof, or ultimate."[36] She notes that she is comfortable using these words because she can point to scientific reactions which offer objective proof of these claims.

Similarly, in response to a listener's question on the Milk Street podcast, Kimball (and co-host Sara Moulton) bemoan older recipes that use terms like "pinch," "dash," "glug," and "splash." He remembers taking a French cooking class in the early 1970s and "almost [getting] thrown out of the class" for demanding to know what a pinch as opposed to a dash of salt was. Kimball suggests that such recipes written in this style are like "the wild, wild West" and promises to investigate whether it can be determined how much liquid is, in fact, contained in a "glug."[37]

Molecular Gastronomy often falls into the same dichotomies of disengagement and the lure of the workmanship of certainty, especially in the process of molecularizing taste. That is, the flavors of food can be abstracted from any particular substance—or food—and recombined in infinite combinations, as with Herve This's "note-by-note" cuisine (see Sutton 2014: 205). This approach promises greater control of perfected, disembodied flavors, separated from culture and history, a reductionist approach if there ever was one, and not in the cooking sense of reduction. It is one that once again sets up a dichotomy between the male expert scientist who can correct the mistakes of the "old wives tales" that mar kitchen practice from the point of view of Herve This.[38] Once again, this is on the "high-end," but the scientization of taste occurs on the "low end" in the history of sensory science's relationship to the food industry in which procedures such as the Spectrum Descriptive Analysis technique "claim the ability to objectively evaluate *all* taste experiences through a system anchored in industrial foods" (Lahne and Spackman 2018: 2). Sarah Tracy (2018) shows how this industry uses umami to create addictive flavors for human consumption, and Alex Blanchette (2020: 220–22) explores how this is expanded to the "palatants" produced from pig viscera, which provide the same experience of predictable desire (perceived by pet owners) in domestic cats, a process that includes cat tasting panels where the cats' response to flavors are evaluated by such signs as "time spent licking the bowl" and "number of times cat stretches itself around the bowl after eating."

Of course, it is not the use of technology itself that is the problem here. Rather it is the tendency to fetishize technology as a way of removing the human element, the craft and skill that we have been concerned with in this chapter. Thus, for example, the Nordic Food Lab, auxiliary of Noma restaurant, is a place where science and a particular sense of experimentation is wedded to ideas about craft that Pye and Ingold would no doubt be at home with.[39] As Arielle Johnson, head of research in Noma's fermentation lab, describes the relationship: "You sometimes hear about scientists working with food and it's like, 'Oh, you're bringing rationality into the creative process.' No, I don't want to bring rationality to the creative process at all, because that would ruin it. Science is not here to tell you what tastes good. Science is here so that you know how stuff works and that in turn lets you be creative with what you have."[40] Head chef Rene Redzepi also stresses the role of risk in the process, where risk is not reduced to the entrepreneurial side—risk of capital—but is embedded in a whole way of life:

> So you have to recognise that you do it because you love learning new things and exploring the world, meeting new people. And then you have to understand that you're asking people to go to work and feel miserable most of the time because that's what failure does to you. It's really tough. How do you create an environment that has a spirit in which that's OK? At Noma, decisions come from the gut, and what we feel is necessary. Having a good balance between work and family and expanding the community, taking lots of risks—you have to be willing to risk everything.[41]

On Kalymnos taste is vital as well, but it is seen as part of mastery, of learning the "tricks" that make one responsive to the total sociomaterial environment in which one acts (see further discussion in chapter 3). This mastery is, in fact, the work of a lifetime and always sways to the vicissitudes and shifts of local reputation within the community. Thus the "risk" of cooking something that does not taste good is like the risk of failed generosity—it can be damaging to one's ongoing sense of self and one's reputation within the community. In other words, there is no "right and wrong" in the sense that *Cooks Illustrated* would have us believe, there is only right and wrong as part of the daily negotiations of one's embeddedness in a deeply shared sensory/social context.

CRAFT AS POLITICS?

Is there a politics of the kind of craft risk that I have been exploring in this chapter? Perhaps, though it does not necessarily fall on clear left-right lines, especially in a contemporary world in which "the Left" sometimes finds itself defending well-functioning government that "the Right" seems happy to abandon. Kathleen Morris (2016) notes that while craft often frames itself as an act of resistance, it has a long history of being subsumed to the larger goals of capitalism; she suggests that it is, indeed, easy to commodify this particular form of dissent (ranging back to William Morris and the Arts and Crafts movement). Lears suggests a longstanding association of craft with a milder form of resistance, the resistance to modern alienation. Focusing on the period after World War II, he notes that "[m]any educators believed that craftsmanship, as a form of creative play, could restore a lost sense of wholeness to the individual psyche and even to society at large." It would "promote 'adjustment' to the demands of 'modern industrial society'" and thus, he argues, potentially lead to its own kind of conformity (Lears 2019: 162).

Within anthropology, Ingold's approach has come in for criticism because it sometimes seems to simply ignore the larger political-economic imperatives under which making, whether hylomorphic or morphogenetic, occurs. Or as Penny Howard puts it, "This approach makes it difficult to understand why human-environment relations in capitalism exist in their particular and devastating contemporary forms, and therefore to change them."[42] No doubt Ingold's work, and some of the briefs for craft discussed in this chapter, take modernity as their foil more than they do capitalism, even if there is perhaps no better example of the abstractions I have been discussing than the ultimate decontextualizing and disembedding of humans from objects in capitalist production and attendant commodity fetishism. No doubt more home cooking of more locally sourced, and thoughtfully produced, foodstuffs on its own will not create a better world, even if it would strike a blow to some of the most malicious corporations on the planet. And, as critics of Michael Pollan's "return to the kitchen" bromides have widely argued, who will be expected to be doing all that cooking anyway? Utopian dreamers might, however, consider updating the early twentieth-century feminist vision of a centralized cooking system that would save what was widely considered drudgery, was still very much "by hand," and distributed throughout cities through pneumatic tubes (Hayden 1982). Would cooperative kitchens like this, which avoid the individualism and commodification of "Blue Apron" and other new products in the pre-prepared cooking market, be enough to save the "workmanship of risk" while easing the burdens on women (and some men)?

And what do politics, then, have to do with the "perfect recipe"? I believe there is a connection between the impulses that design such disembedding schemes to remove human risk and skill in food preparation and what Lorraine Daston (2019) recently refers to as the development of the "perfect rule" as a "delusion which refuses to die." Daston presents the perfect rule as a product of the last few centuries—Western modernity, broadly speaking. This is when we see the development of the idea of rules not as they were seen in the past as models for behavior or action, but as strictly applicable algorithms, designed to remove the necessity to consider exceptions. She notes that prior to the eighteenth century most rules "whether from statecraft or cooking or card games are taught by examples, exceptions, and experience; and they're meant to be applied to a world that is full of surprises and angular particulars" (Daston 2019). I think of these angular particulars when I consider Kalymnians at work with their knives and with recalcitrant ingredients and contingent social and material environments. Indeed, it is notable that Daston reaches for the example of cooking, just as Ingold and Crawford did in their discussion of the different types of and approaches to knowledge they wish to emulate. Perhaps there are few better remedies for the abstractions of modernity than getting our hands dirty in the kitchen, taking a risk, engaging with the contingencies of compliant and recalcitrant, engaging and enticing matter.

CODA

I had just finished writing this chapter when I heard Christopher Kimball's interview with chef Alex Ainouz,[43] a regular guest on the Milk Street Radio program, about sous vide cooking. Ainouz notes that the immersion circulator used for sous vide cooking has gone from a high-end product costing thousands of dollars to something easy to get at less than eighty dollars that will interact with your smartphone: "An app is taking care of the temperature for you, you don't have to do anything no more. Plug it in . . . and wait for perfection to be delivered." Kimball, in his more approachable persona, objects that sous vide is not real cooking. "Do you know why I hate it? Because when I cook, I want to cook. I want to smell the food; I want to mess around with the food. And so, you put it in a plastic bag, and you go watch your iPhone for an hour, I mean, c'mon!" Ainouz responds with a defense of sous vide as meant for all the people who are terrified of entering the kitchen and ruining an expensive cut of meat, who will be encouraged to do so with the guarantee of perfection that sous vide affords. He tells Kimball, "Think of your uncle, your neighbors, your mom, all these guys can now perfectly cook a steak." Ainouz, however, at this point changes tack, worried that a future full of immersion circulators will be one in which the meaning of perfection has been lost, given that it will become so standardized. He wonders if perhaps the idea of perfection that he notes is indeed ubiquitous in our contemporary moment, has become "vastly overrated," and that we should work on "acceptance rather than perfection." He suggests, "There are no risks anymore, no surprises, in this future I think we might have become a bunch of harmless sociopaths." Note here that without elaborating it, he suggests that there is something antisocial about the imposition of perfection through sous vide's anti-cooking cooking. Note also that he is using *risk* in a way close to what I have been arguing for here. It certainly fits with Pye's ideas about standardization as part of the "workmanship of certainty," that Ainouz is suggesting will be provided by a sous vide future. But he also seems to suggest a use of risk to mean deviation from the accepted single standard, and here he retains some of the idea of culinary perfectionism. It is only because we need contrast that constant perfection is a problem, just as we cannot enjoy sunny days if every day is sunny.

So we return to the question of how we understand risk. I have suggested so far several analytical directions to make risk a useful concept for our ethnographic explorations of cooking (and other cultural practices). In the next chapter, I will argue that it is only through seeing *risk* and its related synonyms in cultural terms, seeing how people themselves define the role of contingency in everyday life, that we can gain a holistic understanding of cooking as "everyday risk." But for the moment, I return to the dialogue I have been quoting and note that in this case it is Kimball who comes to the rescue, offering a definition that an anthropologist can live with: "Cooking is not about perfection, it's about cooking. And you don't know exactly what you're going to turn out every time." I could not agree more.

NOTES

1. Sophie Haigney, "Disrupting the Dining Experience?" *Slate*, 22 May 2019. Retrieved 1 December 2020 from https://slate.com/technology/2019/05/virtual-reality-food-changing-dining-experience.html. Glenn Adamson (2013: 73) argues that Pye refuses any association of the workmanship of risk with craft production, a point I will consider further below.

2. An association challenged by sources such as the *Journal of Contemporary Craft*, which even in its title attempts to mitigate the association of craft with the past.

3. Mike Daisey makes this point about the Foxconn factory in Shenjen, China. I do not think it has been invalidated by the subsequent scandal over some of his claims that were made up. See *This American Life* episodes 454 and 460, www.thisamericanlife .org.

4. Suchman 2007. Mike Press notes that "[c]raft presents us with the oldest knowledge there is: the most adaptable, the most fluid knowledge that our culture has produced—knowledge about making things. Wedded to the most contemporary technology, this knowledge is enabling makers to assert a vital new relevance and value for craft" (2007: 264–65).

5. A repetition that is never, in fact, exactly the same (see Portisch 2010).

6. For an excellent summary of Richard Sennett's position contextualized within the broader craft literature, see Paul Harper (2013: 115–17).

7. In typing this on my computer, MS Word autocorrected "craftness" to "craftiness." Indeed. I will have more to say about craftiness in the next chapter.

8. "Drag of material abrasion" is an interesting choice of phrase by Tim Ingold. Elsewhere he notes that materials are "alternately pliant and recalcitrant" (2013: 70). I do not think that Ingold means to suggest that materials are metaphorical drags for creativity, but rather points of engagement.

9. Though see Ingold 2000: 332–34 for a more extended discussion.

10. I must say that while I agree with the sentiment, I think Bruno Latour is a bit unfair to Mr. Spock here, who is, if anything, full of contradictions, a hybrid creature himself.

11. See discussion of Fannie Farmer in Sutton (2006).

12. Giard 1998; Heldke 1992.
13. Kalymnian women did keep some recipes, in my experience, though mostly for making various kinds of baked goods.
14. I will return to the notion of cooking "tricks" as a type of knowledge in the next chapter.
15. See Sutton 2014: 122–23.
16. Helen Rennie, "The Secret to Culinary 'Creativity,'" 13 February 2020. Retrieved 14 February 2020 from https://www.youtube.com/watch?v=W7qYlBEa3-Q&feature =share.
17. Adjusting and assessing, of course, does not need to involve stepping away from the embodied process of cooking and thinking about it as a separate, mental activity, but can be part of the total process, as Geoffrey Gowlland has argued in his work on Taiwanese potters (Gowlland 2017).
18. See Finn 2011. Note that Jacques Pepin is talking about home cooking in this video. The issues raised by professional and restaurant cooking in terms of risk, reproduction, and change are very different from those raised by "everyday cooking" and deserve separate consideration.
19. KQED, "Brussel Sprout Love: Jacques Pépin: More Fast Food My Way | KQED," 16 December 2008. Retrieved 14 February 2020 from https://www.youtube.com/ watch?v=4GokR2C9wy0&t=15m50s.
20. See Trubek et al. (2017: 303) on the importance of thinking of improvisation alongside more typically defined cooking skills.
21. See also Scott 1998; Carrier and Miller 1998.
22. Of course, this is not an invention of neoliberalism but an ongoing project of Western modernity.
23. L.V. Anderson and Christian Lesperance, "The Undisputed Right Way to Chop an Onion," *Slate,* 11 November 2014. Retrieved 14 February 2020 from http://www .slate.com/blogs/browbeat/2014/11/11/how_to_chop_an_onion_the_right_way_ video.html.
24. Modernist cooks seem to fetishize science and technology and ridicule the human, "female" elements of cooking. See Wilson 2012: 257–58. I do not develop gender themes here, but see Sutton 2014, especially chapter 4 and conclusion.
25. Bob Granleese, "Is It Worth Trying Sous-Vide at Home?" *The Guardian,* 3 May 2019. Retrieved 21 April 2021 from https://www.theguardian.com/food/2019/may/03/ is-it-worth-trying-sous-vide-at-home-kitchen-aide.
26. Rebecca Santiago, "Why Food-Obsessed Millennials Suck at Cooking," *New York Post,* 3 October 2017. Retrieved 14 February 2020. https://nypost.com/2017/10/03/ why-food-obsessed-millennials-suck-at-cooking/. One researcher quoted in the article notes: "Offloading robs you of the opportunity to develop the long-term knowledge structures that help you make creative connections, have novel insights and deepen your knowledge," though from what I can tell, this claim was not made based on research on cooking in particular.
27. Mike Murphy, "IBM's AI Computer Has Come Up with Some Pretty Incredible Food Pairings," *Quartz,* 12 April 2015. Retrieved 14 February 2020 from http:// qz.com/381226/ibms-ai-supercomputer-has-come-up-with-some-pretty-incredible-food-pairings/.
28. Eustacia Huen, "The World's First Home Robotic Chef Can Cook over 100 Meals," *Forbes,* 31 October 2016. Retrieved 14 February 2020 from https://www

.forbes.com/sites/eustaciahuen/2016/10/31/the-worlds-first-home-robotic-chef-can-cook-over-100-meals/#541346847228.

29. Quoted in Ibid.
30. Ibid.
31. Sutton 2014: 197.
32. As Finn describes, "The effects of these habits cannot be confined to the domestic. Indeed, the distinction between private and public, and the terms of their interaction, is itself highly questionable" (2011: 514–15).
33. See also my discussion of this in Sutton 2014: 193–95.
34. "BBQ Adventure: Heat And Meat in Gugulethu, Cape Town," *Christopher Kimball's Milk Street*, 26 May 2017, 19:00–21:00. Retrieved 1 December 2020 from https://www.177milkstreet.com/radio/bbq-adventure-heat-and-meat-in-gugulethu-cape-town.
35. The Allusionist Podcast. Episode 103. "Food into Words." 5:25–5:30. Retrieved 14 February 2020 from https://www.theallusionist.org/allusionist/food-into-words?rq=food%20into%20words.
36. Ibid., 6:20.
37. "Hell's French Kitchen: How 7 Days of Cooking Broke Writer Sam Ashworth," *Christopher Kimball's Milk Street*, 24 January 2020, 18:00–20:00. Retrieved 1 December 2020 from https://www.177milkstreet.com/radio/cooking-broke-sam-ashworth. See also Sarah Clapp, "Glug, Splash, Pinch, Dash: How to Decode Culinary Shorthand," *Christopher Kimball's Milk Street*, 16 April 2020. Retrieved 1 December 2020 from https://www.177milkstreet.com/2020/04/glug-splash-pinch-dash-meaning.
38. See Sophia Roosth's discussion (2013: 8).
39. See also Harry West's (2020) comparative work on cheese making, which illustrates how cheese makers find ways to incorporate new technologies either because of various regulations or because they allow for a certain amount of standardization, while still preserving the sense that skill is involved in monitoring these technologies or even in creating their own tools to address new concerns.
40. "Noma's Taste of Tomorrow: Creating the Future of Food," *Slow Food Western Slope*, 19 February 2016. Retrieved 14 February 2020 from https://slowfoodwesternslope.org/noma-taste-tomorrow-creating-future-food/.
41. Ibid.
42. Howard 2018: 64; see also Sutton 2017.
43. "Cork Dorks: Inside the High-Stakes World of Sommeliers," *Christopher Kimball's Milk Street*, 30 August 2019, 44:00–52:00. Retrieved 1 December 2020 from https://www.177milkstreet.com/radio/cork-dorks-sommeliers-bianca-bosker.

CHAPTER 3

"TO STEAL A BAD HOUR FROM DEATH"

Subjective Risk and Contingent Temporalities in the Greek Kitchen

If you try to play around with the classic recipe, you take a risk. I had done this in the past, to create something using the same ingredients as moussakas. The classical recipe is one, it's the moussakas everyone knows. The risk is that all of us who know moussakas and have associated it in our mind with a memory . . . if that is mother's, grandmother's, father's, family's and it is very hard to take that out of people's minds and say: this moussakas that I am serving you now is better.

—Athens Chef

—We won't have a ruler beside us, [measure] with the eye.
—Yes, with the eye is better, just to give you an idea how big it is.
—Because cooking is the craft of improvisation, and we need to take a bit of risk, we can't sit around measuring grams and centimeters and such.

—SBS Radio Cooking Show host and chef discussing making kadaifi dough for little cheese pies (*tyropitakia*)

You can cut your hand on this!

—Katerina Kardoulia commenting on the can of tomato paste that she just opened with an "old-fashioned" blade can opener

SUBJECTIVE RISK

In the previous two chapters, I argued for two different approaches to risk when analyzing cooking: the risk of categories put in play in each reproduction of "the same" dish and the workmanship of risk that Pye and others have argued is at the heart of a kind of skilled practice based on human creativity rather than mechanical reproduction. Both of those approaches are important, I think, in combining cognitive and embodied approaches to understanding cooking as a kind of everyday risk. But both take an outsider's approach, understanding risk as something that can be analyzed through the observation of practice in various forms. In this final substantive chapter, I turn to understanding subjective risk: the way that cooks themselves frame cooking and experience it as a kind of risk, as well as the cultural values that may go into the idea that risk in cooking (and in other aspects of life) might, or might not, be something that should be sought out because it does (or does not) bring rewards. From the outset, I want to make it clear that, in Greece, cooks do experience cooking as risk, and they see this risk as productive of values and identities (i.e., good food, good cook). In other words, because cooking is so important, Greeks (mostly women) are willing to take (culturally defined) risks to create memorable meals (Sutton 2001:chap. 4). Thus, risk-taking has an existential quality to it.

In the first quote, we see the admission of an Athenian chef tasked explicitly with being creative, but recognizing the potential risk involved in trying to convince his patrons that moussaka is something that can be experimented with and that there is even the possibility of making a better moussaka than the one associated with home and family. In this first instance, risk has a mildly negative valence, recognizing that one's task is difficult. Here we see risk in Sahlins's sense, that is, that the risk that the dish prepared by the chef will not fit, or will fit in an unfavorable way, into the previously established category.

In the second example, we come much closer to the risk explored in chapter 2: the rejection of precision provided by exact measurement and the commitment to using one's own body as the tool of assessment (in this case, "the eye"). Here it is notable that risk is being used in a more positive sense; as the radio announcer suggests, it is worth the risk, because if we spend all our time worrying about grams and centimeters then something essentially human, or perhaps better essentially Greek, will be lost, a point I'll argue further below.

My third example comes from my fieldwork on everyday cooking on Kalymnos. It involves an older Kalymnian woman, Katerina Kardoulia, who has an internal dialogue in the midst of opening a can of tomato paste on the

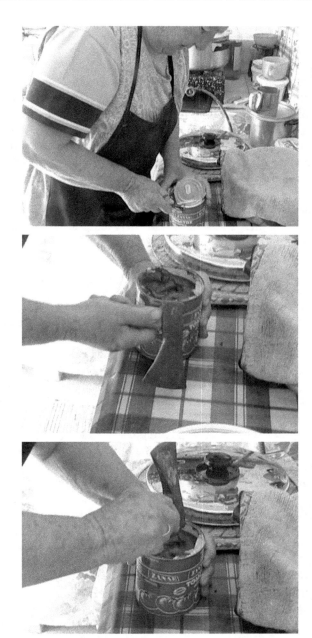

Figures 3.1, 3.2, and 3.3. Katerina Kardoulia using her "traditional" can opener (and a hammer usually used for leatherworking) to open a can of tomato paste. © David Sutton.

risks and benefits of "traditional" and "new" can openers as represented by the choices and preferences of herself and her daughter.

As I analyzed (Sutton 2014: 61–63), Katerina recognizes that her choice of a blade can opener creates problems that need to be addressed and potential risks she mitigates by hammering the spikes back down along the side of the can.[1] While admitting the advantages of the can opener that her daughter bought, she insists that it doesn't suit her and with satisfaction notes, "I'm very traditional, a traditionalist." Katerina poses the decision to use the blade can opener as a matter of skill: "When I am with the new can opener, I am not a skillful person." But it is also as an existential choice, in this particular instance over whether to follow the moderns or the traditionalists, very much like the Athenian chef quoted at the beginning of this chapter. In embracing the can opener, Katerina is also embracing the risk that insists that cooking, like other things that involve risk, is an open-ended but ultimately rewarding practice.

In this chapter I will combine all of these approaches to subjective risk by trying to get at some of the cultural underpinnings of the attitudes I've been describing. Roughly six years later, I observed Katerina opening several cans of tomatoes that no longer required a can opener because the lid could be simply removed with a pull ring.

She joked about how the need for her old can opener had been largely obviated, noting that she had "modernized." However, as discussed in the previous chapter, the loss of one technique is usually replaced by another, and Katerina did not feel that the need for skill and risk in the kitchen was any less than before.

Risk, in Sahlins's sense of "risk of categories," exists everywhere, but how we value it is culturally variable. And this links to the way people perceive history and change. We can see this in Sahlins's work, in which he uses the notion of "subjective risk"[2] to show that historical actors may use categories for their own purposes or as part of their own particular projects, to which the categories, again, may or may not correspond. Thus, in his famous Captain Cook arriving in Hawaii example, he recognizes that beyond the shared set of categories that are put at risk in acts of reference, differently situated actors such as Hawaiian priests, royalty, commoners, and women may use the categories—or challenge them—in pursuit of their own subjective projects. I take this to be an argument about the cultural nature of historical consciousness, an idea that he develops in other writings (Sahlins 1985: chap. 3) to suggest that "different cultures constitute their own mode of historical action, consciousness, and determination—their own historical practice." Sahlins contrasts what he sees as "heroic history" of "kings and battles" in Fiji, which "shows an unusual capacity for sudden change or rupture: a mutation of the cultural course" (1985: 41), with Ilongot historicity in which people

Figures 3.4 and 3.5 Katerina Kardoulia opening the newfangled can. © David Sutton.

"act on the sense that they invent their own social lives, each generation as it were rediscovering the Philippines" (1985: 53). He also suggests that, in the United States, there is a similar sense of history as the result of "the institutional sum of individual actions," though in this case regulated through "the marketplace" (1985: 52). I would note (and Sahlins indeed seems at times to point to this) the idea that this is a hegemonic view, and there may be multiple subjective notions of historicity in play.

The point of this elaboration is to suggest that cultural ideas about the relationship between recipe and meal, or the value of improvisation and reproduction, are part of the process by which an event is defined as an event rather than a happening; in other words, while the risk of categories is inherent in all human semiosis according to Sahlins, the evaluation of the results can be culturally variable. For some societies, all action is imagined as ideally sui generis, while for others it is a reinstantiation of the actions of ancestors. All societies, as Stephan Palmié and Charles Stewart (2016: 209) note, "differ in their openness to the idea of historical change: some encourage it, others suppress it—not the facts of change, but the idea of it." For my purposes people in Greece may embrace historicities associated with Western modernity while still experiencing daily life in terms of other historicities that at first sight might be considered "non-modern." Indeed, these perspectives coexist (Hamilakis 2008). How people talk about continuity and change in cooking practices is obviously an important aspect of understanding these historicities in everyday life. By the same token, anthropologists should be aware of the ways people may hide change in continuity and vice versa, in the pursuit of what Sahlins calls their particular "subjective projects." In Kalymnos, I dubbed this attitude toward continuity and change "analogic thinking," an attitude that constantly scans the present for signs of a past that is similar, though not identical; that is, a perspective that recognizes events as both continuity and repetition of the past as well as change, or what I called "repetition with difference" (Sutton 1998: chaps. 5–6).

APPROACHING EVERYDAY RISK

However, analogic thinking and orientation to the past notwithstanding, in Greece one might also see a culture in which moments of rupture might, in fact, be explicitly thematized given a general cultural focus on the role of risk in everyday life. Here is a case in which "heroic history," in Sahlins's terms, is lived by many ordinary people (the implications of the generalization of this history to the wider population is an interesting ethnographic question). A number of anthropologists working in Greece have described a cultural attitude in which contingency is seen not as something to be avoided, but as part of what makes life meaningful. For example, Michael Herzfeld developed his notion of a "poetics of manhood" in Greece, in which "the ability to improvise, to make the most of whatever chance offers, is the mark of the true man" (Herzfeld 1985: 135). And, "Glendiot [Cretan] men rejoice in the very uncertainty of their lives, since it [is] this that gives them the chance to demonstrate their improvisational skills" (1985: 135). Thomas Malaby, who studied gambling in Crete, came to similar conclusions: "in dealing with the pervasive indeterminacies of experience, risk . . . rather than tamed and quantified, is engaged and performed" (2003: 21).[3] And in my own earlier work I described the satisfaction that Kalymnian men got from their life-threatening involvement with dynamite-throwing, revealing an existential attitude that dismisses concern for certain kinds of risk (Sutton 1998). Kalymnian men also took a certain pride in engaging risk that

was less voluntary than dynamite throwing, particularly in the sponge industry, where they faced constant risks of injury or death. While the sponge
industry was almost extinct at the time I conducted fieldwork on Kalymnos,
Kalymnian men pointed to the fact that they had, in some cases, replaced
sponge diving with occupations like bridge painting (for those who had mi-
grated), which required the same death-defying courage as their previous
storied profession.[4]

All of these cases involved male performances. However, work on Greek
sexuality by Alexandra Halkias (2004) and Heather Paxson (2004) explores
some of the ways that risk is as productive in women's willingness to pursue
sexual relationships without contraception. Paxson notes that, perhaps unsurprisingly, risk can "heighten sexual desire." It also allows Greek women
to evaluate their partners, to see whether they are driven purely by desire, or
are willing to take the responsibility of providing protection, and thus prove
themselves responsible partners. Paxson thus argues that embracing risk
provides a kind of "strategy and agency," while not explicitly "advancing the
cause of feminism" (2004: 149). Such an approach is also, much like Malaby's
male gamblers, associated with an embrace of chance over calculation, the
latter being seen as a Western, "modern" attitude that makes for more sterile
sexual relations (Paxson 2004: 149). Halkias similarly refers to the "sponta-
neity" and "Greek freeness of spirit" associated with the risk of unprotected
sex (2004: 195, 198), which is contrasted with the calculation and counting
(as in the "rhythm method") associated with modernity. Thus, sexual risk
can be seen as similar to the "practices" that Michel de Certeau and Luce
Giard highlighted, tactics that resist the rationalization of modernity.

One might want to view these as the kind of dangerous risks that sociol-
ogists label "edgework." However, in studying Kalymnian cooking, I found
that women expressed similar attitudes toward the admittedly more mundane and measured risks involved in cutting a loaf of bread while holding it
against one's chest. This example fits nicely with that of Katerina and the can
opener, except to the extent that the former is more part of an unchallenged
habitus than a practice that is explicitly commented upon (Sutton 2014:
191–92). It fits as well with the willingness to try something new against a
background of familiarity, thus "taking a risk" of a spoiled meal (and dam-
aged reputation). As with these other examples, here women did not see
risk as something to be mitigated by improved tools or techniques, but to be
productively engaged as part of an existential attitude toward life. Indeed,
as discussed in the previous chapter, this fits with the notion that contingency should be explicitly embraced as part of what makes cooking, in fact,
cooking.

Stavroula Pipyrou, commenting on her observations of women in the village that she grew up in (Kalloni, Northern Greece), suggested that there

was always a desire to mix "imagination" and "economy" in cooking (*fantasia, oikonomia*).[5] This was expressed in the dish *tourlou*, a kind of thrown together dish made from whatever vegetables were available in the garden (typically some combination of potatoes, peppers, and zucchini). It was a dish that involved risk because it might suggest to neighbors that you were too bored or too poor to cook a "proper" meal.[6] And, if you added the wrong quantity and combination of ingredients, it might even be inedible. So the risk was to wrest flavor out of this dish. But its unscripted nature also allowed for all kinds of imagination. Pipyrou's grandmother often used wild coriander in making this dish, a flavor that was quite different—some would call it "unnatural" (*afisiko*)—but that she liked quite a lot. Her grandmother also sometimes used a preserved wild plum (*koromilo*) jam to add a sweet-and-sour flavor to the dish. But each time it would be a little different, drawing on imagination and economy to overcome contingency and create the surprise of a flavorful combination. "She would want a bit of difference (*ego tha to kano* allios! [I will do it *otherwise*!]). There were other women like her in the village who would trust their own preferences."[7]

In the time that I have been doing research on Kalymnos, a major change has been that risk is no longer simply attendant on tools, ingredients, or other social challenges (how to feed ten people who show up unexpectedly, for example), but on one's openness to change and alteration in recipes and ingredients. One Kalymnian woman in her fifties told me how she first saw Greek eggplant salad (*melitzanosalata*, similar to what in the United States is called babaganoush) at a restaurant that she visited for a wedding celebration. She thought at the time that it looked like vomit. But after seeing it more often and observing a friend preparing it when she was staying on Rhodes, she started to make it for her family, noting "we took the risk." Risk here is seen as a willingness to prepare something completely new, in this case, though with familiar ingredients and familiar flavors. It is also to continue to learn new ways of preparing the familiar, or variations on traditional recipes, perhaps comparable to the attitude expressed by the Athenian chef in the first epigraph to this chapter. The risk, again, involves a potentially spoiled meal, and, perhaps, ridicule by family members and/or outsiders, which is not something to be laughed off given the importance placed on everyday taste that I documented on Kalymnos.

Engaging with contingency, however, comes more commonly in the form not of embracing brand new recipes, but discovering new techniques to improve upon the execution of familiar dishes, which may eventually have long-term impacts.[8] For example, Stavroula Pipyrou, observing her grandmother again, said that women of her generation who had lived through World War II and the Greek Civil War were especially eager and happy to embrace novelty in cooking. Her grandmother would make an orange cake that was served at memorials for the dead (*mnimosina*). She didn't change the ingredients, "but [changed] the rhythm of inserting the ingredients and the order. And the way she was beating the eggs (she was so strong)." Everyone talked about her version of the cake, even though the idea for the changes had not come from her but from a "silly, younger woman." Her cake, then, transformed from an unremarkable repetition of a familiar dish, or a "happening," into an "event."

TRICKS AND PATENTS: ATTITUDES TOWARD CONTINGENCY

One of the key aspects of being a good cook is to be able to respond to contingency with improvisation and/or innovation. I stress at the outset that this takes culturally specific forms, though with dimensions that beg for cross-cultural comparison. As with any "happening," Robin Wagner-Pacifici argues, it usually must take on certain predetermined forms in order to become an "event" and to be distinguishable from "ground" or background. Speaking of events that impact identities, she notes: "Events are restless. Identities can come and go; our ability to see them depends on the forms in which they appear [and] the affordances of those forms" (2017: 113). What are the "forms" of Greek improvisation and innovation? In Greek cooking, innovations in relation to contingency are typically known as "tricks" or *kolpa* (singular *kolpo*), or "patents" (*patendes,* singular *patenda*). *Kolpa* are the small adjustments, embodied or explicit, by which one negotiates everyday problems, challenges, and contingencies in food preparation. They range from special methods to improve flavor, such as boiling one's Greek coffee several times after pouring the valued foam into the coffee cup so that the coffee doesn't taste weak (see Sutton 2014: 216), to storing herbs in the freezer so that one does not run out. Some people have a *kolpo* of putting a piece of cotton dipped in vinegar on a pot of boiling cauliflower to prevent the house from smelling like cauliflower. Or to avoid having a dense meatball, some Greeks refrain from squeezing too tightly the liquid-soaked bread they put in the mince.[9] *Kolpa* typically take the form illustrated in the above examples of averting or avoiding some potential bad outcome. They need not be difficult.[10] Tricks are not common knowledge; they are by their nature something that only some people are aware of. So, removing the skin from tomatoes in a stew would not be a "trick," it is simply a variation that some people prefer while others do not (Sutton 2014: 46).

What is the difference between tricks and *patendes* (lit. patents)?[11] As my colleague, Leonidas Vournelis, put it to me:

while both tricks and patents are applicable when one bypasses the usual or pre-
scribed way of doing things (in and out of the kitchen, in all walks of life), the latter
emphasizes the individual's ability to move successfully outside paradigms of action;
innovation is a characteristic of both *kolpa* and *patendes*, however, *kolpa* narrows the
focus on the innovative act, which typically refers to knowledge picked up from another person; *patendes* refer both to the innovative act and to the person as an innova-
tor, someone who came up herself with a new way of doing things.[12]

Another way to think about "tricks" versus "patents" is that patents are
typically discovered in the moment as one tries to get around a particular
problem. Anthropologist Neni Panourgia (2009) described the difference as
follows: a trick is something that you know how to do to make something
different, like using yoghurt instead of milk in béchamel sauce to make it
more healthy. It is something that might be acknowledged by the person
eating your food: "what trick did you use to do this?" A patent is a way of
solving a particular emergent problem.

Such as the crisis when your mayonnaise has separated and you don't
have more eggs, oil, and mustard, so you come up with the idea of warm-
ing and stirring the mayonnaise in a double boiler for long enough that the
ingredients bind themselves together again. Or, as in my moussaka example
from the previous chapter, making sure that an undesired result such as a
sauce overflowing the dish does not occur. This shows that there might be a
different temporality to patents than to tricks. Panourgia notes a similar distinction to that made by Vournelis: "*Patenda* is to do with thinking outside
the box, not bending the system. *Kolpo* is to do with gaming the system."[13]
Stavroula Pipyrou compared her own experience with *kolpa* in cooking with
her fieldwork on dancing Tarantella in Calabria, Italy. As she put it: "*Kolpo* is
like the strike (*ktipima*; in dancing). It requires cunning. When you cook you
have to risk a strike (*ktipima*). Every time women were using a *kolpo*, they
were attacking, in order to take something ordinary and make it extraordinary. The risk to go beyond the recipe."[14]

The distinction, then, between tricks and patents is that they address different kind of risks. Tricks may be like a strike, but they are also, as this last
example suggests, planned. They address "known unknowns" or risks that
can be anticipated. Patents are about addressing "unknown unknowns" (the
popularization of the latter concept being perhaps Donald Rumsfeld's sole
contribution to humanity). They require an attitude that anticipates not just
the embrace of risk, but the fact that things are so often unpredictable. It
is interesting to compare the forms of *kolpa* and *patendes* with related concepts described in other cultural contexts. For example, Meredith Abarca,
in writing about Mexican cooks, describes what she calls *chistes* or twists,
which she claims are ways of asserting agency on the part of some women.
As she puts it, "when people add their own *chiste* (twist) to the preparation

Figure 3.6. Katerina Kardoulia figured out this as a method to soften cheese that had become too hard to grate while boiling water for some other use. In the moment, it is a *patenda*; over time it becomes a *kolpo*. © David Sutton.

of a recipe, they add their knowledge and creative expression to it. *Chistes* . . . represent moments of asserting acts of agency" (Abarca 2006: 4). This often comes in the face of discourses of authenticity that come from authority fig-ures (such as TV cooking show chefs) or from the wider community of cooks. She noted one woman who had a *chiste* for making enchiladas (unfortunately the specifics of the *chiste* are not described). She was told by other women "'those are not enchiladas' . . . To such a response Contreras replies . . . I know how I like them and how to make them" (2006: 4). For Abarca, *chistes* can be seen as elements of style or "creative energy." This places them closer to *patendes*, perhaps, than to *kolpa*; although as I have been suggesting, whether dubbed tricks or patents, they are as much about circumventing particular sociomaterial circumstances as they are about channeling creative energy.[15]

An interesting related term that can be found in cooking discourse is *mis-tiko* or secret (pl. *mistika*). In some ways *mistiko* can be a synonym for *kolpo*, as when one refers to "my secrets" (*ta mistika*) one can be discussing the same range of procedures designated by *kolpa*. Though in calling them "my secrets" one draws explicit attention to their circulation or non-circulation, and how that might be managed, as I discuss in relation to the notion of artisans in the next section. In other words, a *kolpo* is something easily re-vealed, while a *mistiko* is something that might only be revealed after estab-lishing trust, if at all. "The *mistiko*, you don't share it, so that others don't copy it."[16] Secrets are different from tricks in another way. They suggest a different notion of agency and materiality in relation to foods, that is, in highlighting the fact that food itself may hold secrets. A trick or patent is a direct human activity. A secret implies a certain activity, but its "activeness" is more implicit (and it often implies something complicated). The "secret of chickpeas"—they remain hard unless you employ various tricks to soften them—is something that must be learned over time, sometimes acquired through verbal instruction, sometimes "stolen" through observation, as part of one's valued stock of cooking knowledge. The secret of chickpeas, again, implies a demand for tricks (or possibly patents), that one must understand first, and then act upon. An implication here is that food does not reveal its secrets easily, it has its own autonomy that one must find ways to accommodate, similar to my discussion of Matthew Crawford's notion of the need for engagement with an autonomous, recalcitrant world as a way of putting ourselves at risk (2015: 187). An interesting related phrase is *ta mistika tou eppagelmatos* or tricks of the trade. Both the secrets of *revithia* and of the trade imply a public recognition of the tacit knowledge that must be sussed out and eventually incorporated in the process of becoming knowledgeable.[17]

Malaby's study of gambling in Crete resonates with this material in describing an attitude toward chance that challenges "official" ideas about risk management and minimization and pervades the ordinary and the existential. Indeed, he takes examples from both the domain of pouring and carrying a cup of coffee without letting it spill ("You must look forward. Only. The cup is nothing. Nothing! Only then will it not spill" [2003: 134]) and facing the existential contingency of one's never-knowable death. He notes that dancing the notorious Greek male dance *zebekeiko* "calls for a convincing presentation of oneself as always on the brink of disaster (about to fall) yet at the last minute able to snatch success (regaining balance) out of the jaws of capricious fate" (2003: 141). Of course, this takes not just attitude, but skill, just as, in the kitchen, one must learn proper skill as well as attitude. When twelve-year-old Kalymnian Katerina was making her first dish, a zucchini omelet, she struggled to cut the zucchini into small pieces, commenting to her mother, "It didn't come out right." Her mother's immediate response was "don't talk nonsense," not to suggest that she hadn't done a good job, but rather that she had said something meaningless—a dish can turn out right or wrong at the end, but in the middle of cooking one never has success or failure, only the possibility of fixing or recuperating one's trick or coming up with a patent in the moment.[18] Indeed, when one woman used the unusual phrase "housewife swindles" (*kombines tis nikokyras*) to refer to one of her tricks, it seemed to index exactly that ability to recover in the middle of cooking, thus creating excellent tasteful food despite myriad contingencies of time, materials, and social demands.

EXISTENTIAL ARTISANS

There is the sense, in Wagner-Pacifici's terms, that patents and tricks are the "forms" that happenings are fit into to make them more enduring, but also that "events" are very much, as they are for Malaby's Cretan gamblers, about assigning identities. In many parts of Greece, a *mastoras* (m) or *mastorissa* (f) is a person who is proficient in their craft, and the terms apply to activities in and out of the household. A *mastoras/mastorissa* knows the tricks of their trade, or the *kolpa* that allow one to excel in one's endeavors; these *kolpa* are picked up by the person, as one learns over time how to become proficient, However, when a *mastoras/mastorissa* comes up with their own unique way of doing something, it is often referred to as a *patenda*. One's ability to come up with a *patenda* on the spot and thus deal with unanticipated contingencies helps construct the person's social identity as a *mastoras*. The *mastoras* is not just someone who knows. He or she is someone who excels in embodying and applying techniques. The *mastoras* again does not erase risk, but— like the image of the craftsman discussed in the last chapter—understands how to embrace it and manage it successfully. *Mastoras* or *mastorissa* can be a term of recognition; that is, if someone executes something well, others will call them *mastorissa* to recognize their accomplishment. Over time, the term may stick.[19] Thus skilled acts must be circulated in the community to make one's reputation known. In the same way, sharing one's trick or patent, thereby moving it from the realm of one's secrets (*ta mistika mou*) to that of common knowledge is a way of building one's reputation. Once, a woman showed me her cache of frozen wild herbs that she had saved from the summer to use in a bean soup. She then described how a younger woman had praised her for this idea, saying "you're a real school with all that could be learned from following you." This also points to the fact that, just as "secrets" can be shared, risk can be collective. While I've been pointing to the individual tricks and patents of particular Kalymnian women, it is important to note that these always play out in a context of family, community, and island. Just as taste is a collective project in what I call "robust food cultures" (Sutton 2016b), so can one find many examples of mothers, daughters, and granddaughters working together and sharing risk. They might share (sometimes grudgingly) the appreciation of success, as well as the blame for failure. This explains the mutual tasting of dishes while they are cooking, as well as the constant sharing of prompts (how many eggs to add to a béchamel sauce, for example) between mother and daughter. As Evdokia Passa put it to me, when explaining why she consults her mother on amounts and ingredients in recipes that they've both made many times, "Even though I pretty much know, I prefer to ask, so I can say if it doesn't turn out right 'you told me'" (Sutton 2014: 116). Such practices are built into a "sensory regime" (Howes

2003) in which taste, smell, and synesthethetic combinations are prioritized and are constant sources of conversation and commentary among non-cooks as well as cooks.[20]

As noted, these practices of confronting contingency are not restricted to the domain of cooking. On the contrary, they are part of a larger cultural thematics that stresses the ways life is a struggle against many obstacles, and one must be constantly ready to improvise to face these obstacles. In Greece, there is a tradition of agonistic relations between the state and its citizens. Strict and often violently imposed austerity policies foisted upon an unwilling populace are only the latest example. Herzfeld (1992, 1997) has extensively investigated this complex set of relations between the Greek state and the Greek people and documented a number of resistance strategies adopted by Greeks when engaging with their government that often involve subterfuge, evasion, and occasionally open defiance.

While de Certeau, Giard, and Mayol in *The Practice of Everyday Life Volume 2* do not provide the kind of detailed ethnographic examples that could be grounds for comparison, it is notable that they see cooking as among the tactics used by ordinary people to resist the powerful standardization forces of "modernity," as discussed in the previous chapter. De Certeau indeed suggests that "tricks" are a key aspect of the resistance that he is attempting to document. As he writes: "Dwelling, moving about, speaking, reading, shopping and cooking are activities that seem to correspond to tactical ruses and surprises: clever tricks of the 'weak' within the order established by the 'strong,' an art of putting one over on the adversary on his own turf, hunter's tricks, maneuverable, polymorph mobilities, jubilant, poetic and warlike discoveries" (1984: 40). Here, though, it is not clear if he is taking the perspective of the analyst or of her subjects.

In Greece, Herzfeld, as noted, has made similar arguments for contingency and improvisation as resistance, though more specifically against the authority of the state and official versions of lived experience. He argues that Cretan shepherds see life as "a struggle" and the goal of improvisatory practice is to "steal a bad hour from death" (1985: 149), suggesting the temporal ruses that are very much part of the kitchen tricks I've been discussing, as well as the existentially risky aspects of confrontations with contingency—it is death that you are attempting to steal from, after all. In telling stories or composing oral poetry (*mantinadhes*), Cretan shepherds seek the risk of an improvisatory move that may either be judged as successful or potentially as unsuccessful and thus deemed to be the work of a "hack." It is thus by challenging conventions in a recognizable manner that a man succeeds "in the degree to which a man can present his own deviations from the stock manner as an improvement" by having "chanced upon" a successful move, rather than having pondered a response in advance (1985: 140), thus having made "effective use of opportunity" (1985: 148).

While Herzfeld, like Malaby, argues that this is what defines Cretan rural manhood, in relation to a more middle-class, bureaucratic urban ethos, I would argue that Kalymnian cooking shares many of these traits of grasping upon opportunity and stretching convention through the adoption of tricks and patents. In the case of women, it is partly their own reputation that is being defended. But in the context of a modernity that offers increasing commodification and fast-food options, diminution of taste, tacit knowledge, and other sensory aspects of place, it is the potential social death brought by modernity, neoliberalism, and austerity that these claims to value creation through risk attempt to resist.

C. Nadia Seremetakis provides numerous examples of loss of taste as a symptom of modernity, including her much cited loss of the peach variety "the breast of Aphrodite" to the standardized, indistinguishable "peach" (1994: 1). As she puts it, deeply embedded tasting practices are one example of those resistances which "aim to redress the body that is fragmented and sensorially turned against itself by the shock structures of modernity." More recently, Seremetakis (2019) writes how, during the financial crisis, olive oil extracted from one's own trees "has (re)appeared in everyday life as a metaphor of an emergent topophilia (love of place). The previously neglected practice of extracting oil from 'your own olive trees' now promises to restore touchability" (2019: 168). Once again, she contrasts this with the sensory anonymity of TV cooking shows cut off from any recognizable tradition of "secrets" (*mistika*) and shared tastes. In my ongoing research on Kalymnos (see Sutton 2016b), I have been tracing the rediscovery of certain foods associated with the past that are part of tacit knowledge, the recovery of which allows Kalymnians to survive in crisis times. Such dishes include things like spoon sweets (*glika tou koutaliou*) as a cheaper homemade alternative to bakery goods and a way of preserving available fruits and vegetables. They also include pork preserved in fat and salt (*kavourmas*), which was associated with Kalymnos's sponge diving past (because it could be taken on boats and kept without refrigeration), and which some suggested could help Kalymnians through the economic crisis when even sources of electricity were no longer guaranteed. These foods have a temporality; they are preserved, take a long time to cook, and can be kept for a long time. Once again, Seremetakis contrasts foods that "take a journey of maturation which cannot be captured by television time" (2019: 169).

This raises questions of how cooking risk can be related to questions not just of embracing contingency but of experiencing temporality. One common expression that friends use in Greece upon parting is "good continuity," or "successful continuation" (*kali synehia*), a phrase that became much more prevalent in the years since the Crisis.[21] Though not necessarily about food, the phrase suggests that whatever endeavor you are in the midst of may pose challenges, or the type of unknown contingencies I've been discussing. Thus, the expression offers a hope/wish that you are able to face the challenges and contingencies that, during the time of the Crisis, even the most ordinary activities pose.

I also examined the example of a politician—the Deputy Minister of Social Solidarity under the Syriza government in 2015—who tried to make a claim about the ability of ordinary Greeks to face contingency by making stuffed vegetables, a common dish that, while highly regarded, also has the associations of making something from whatever you have available. It is a good example of a food for hard times, and this is what the minister intended by referring to this dish. However, she received many negative responses because her remark seemed to suggest shared suffering, when clearly she was not suffering herself. The comment made public the histories by which ordinary people get by, but which should not be called out in public, particularly by someone who is not among the struggling. I stress this again as a reminder of the ways that cooking can be related to larger concerns about temporality and risk: in this case, the ability to have "good continuity" involves the kind of cultural intimacy that Herzfeld has stressed as a part of Greek self-knowledge, but not necessarily self-representation for outsiders (Herzfeld 1997).

RISK, COOKING, AND HISTORICAL CONSCIOUSNESS

In my earlier work on food and memory (Sutton 2001: chap. 4), I argued that one of the mechanisms for remembering meals on Kalymnos was the fact that meals were highly structured and fairly predictable on a weekly basis, but that people marked out that predictability with "unusual" elements that represented "variations on a theme," a view of meals that derived from Mary Douglas's (1974) work on meal structures. Thus, people kept track of their meals, to the extent that they did, by noting the ways that each particular meal was both similar to, and different from, the expected pattern.

I further argued that local historical consciousness took a parallel form, whereby history was seen to follow recognizable patterns, and in which events could be narrated for their convergence and divergence with these patterns, history manifesting as "repetition with difference." At a local level, furthermore, the word "history" was pluralized to "histories," which often referred to the potentially embarrassing stories that broke the calm of mundane time with a disruptive event. These narratives could also be positive, as with stories of one's food-based generosity that were key to creating a highly valued, generous reputation. As I wrote, "For Kalymnians, 'history,' like the meal, is constituted by events organized around certain accepted themes (structures) that break up the flow of everyday life in which 'nothing happens' . . . If 'History' on the national level is contrasted to periods of time when nothing happens, local level 'histories' are explicitly contrasted to actions that simply 'pass the day' uneventfully" (Sutton 2001: 116). In revisiting these ideas, I would make certain additions and appendages in relation to my current argument. The first is to note that, in some ways, "tricks" and "patents" are the forms such variations take; in a culture in which taste matters, they are the variations on a theme that are endlessly discussed. Second, one thing my earlier discussion did not make explicit enough is how the notions of everyday "subjective" risk that I have laid out here fit into the way historical consciousness is understood. That is, while I suggested that in some cases "passing the day" without comment is a successful strategy to avoid creating negative "histories" for oneself or one's family, I also showed that people actively seek out variations—by foraging for extra ingredients, varying their cooking methods, and making other small changes to mark out the meal as special or memorable. Thus, like Herzfeld's sheep thieves creating poetic variations on the structure of theft narratives, Kalymnians find ways to improvise within the accepted structure of proper meals and proper tastes. They take the risk, knowing that a failed meal is also the source of comment and potential gossip.

Finally, since I wrote some of these ideas, a considerable literature has emerged exploring various dimensions of Greek historical consciousness.[22] Much of this work challenges the linear view of the past that has been dominant in the academic field of history since the nineteenth century, showing how even in so-called Western societies, linear history coexists with alternative understandings of the past.[23] In exploring Greek historical consciousness, various approaches have challenged linear understandings by suggesting the ways the past can surprise the present, such as "flashing up in a moment of danger," to use Walter Benjamin's suggestive expression. Stewart quotes Benjamin in focusing on the "uncanny," "sudden and surprising," and "spontaneous" surfacing of the past in "a particular moment of social potential" (2017: 138). Social potential should remind us of Herzfeld's shepherds, Malaby's gamblers, and my cooks as they each grasp the opportunities or possibilities that are presented to them. For Stewart this comes in the form of dreams of buried icons in his work on Naxos, in which the icons "[call] out to be unearthed," in a "surprising intervention of the past in the life of the community" (2017: 138). While this suggests an agency that escapes human control, Nicholas Argenti, on the other hand, describes the way the past is made use of in confronting what may be experienced as helplessness "in the tempests of unfolding history" (2019: 268). That is, "we" (Greeks from the island of Chios, in this case) decide "what moments in time to constitute as an event or as a repetition, and to identify what recursions connect one phase of our lives to another and what occurrences are redolent of what others" (2019: 268). This statement resonates with Sahlins's and Wagner-Pacifici's ideas about event-making, as well as my own thoughts on "analogic thinking as history," in which Kalymnians scan the past for parallels to happenings in the present (Sutton 1998: chap. 6).

For these ethnographers, food comes in to play in the context of the current Greek economic crisis that began in 2009. Daniel Knight, for example, takes inspiration from Michel Serres in describing a "folded" or "topographic" understanding of history, in which certain moments from the past can suddenly seem close and feel revived in contemporary crisis times, particularly those from the Greek Civil War. People recall the hunger of wartime and bring back practices of provisioning and hoarding that are suddenly refreshed into everyday consciousness. As Knight, quoting Serres, describes:

> Whereas other entwined histories can be eradicated or forgotten, "percolating through time rather than getting caught in the filter," food retains an extraordinary place in the weaving of social memory, history and artefact. Invested with sensory memory, even the abstract concept of food, employed as a transformative idiom rather than an object itself, incorporates social experience. It is transmitted as a cultural code, as a "constant contemporary," assembled at each moment according to the continuous social fluctuations in the process of time. (Knight 2012: 368)

Thus Knight suggests the power of food, both as a cultural idiom and in its association with episodic memory, to bring past moments to life in the present, often—like Stewart's dreams—in unexpected ways. Argenti similarly notes that, in moments of crisis, history is experienced as repeating: "while people queued up for food at the soup kitchens for the first time since World War II [during the economic crisis of the 2010s] they remembered with visceral force the Great Famine of 1941–43, one crisis effectively collapsing into another—past into present and present into future" (Argenti 2019: 270).

All of these examples focus on the role of the past in times of crisis, though Knight in particular nods to the ways that food is embedded in a cultural code that has everyday as well as extraordinary dimensions. I would like to emphasize the ways that these alternative historicities or forms of historical consciousness have their mundane, everyday applications just as much as they color moments of crisis. An older Kalymnian woman handing a slice of watermelon to her grown son to be eaten without a fork and plate says, "like in the old times," an everyday moment that flashes up from the past just as much as it might in moments of crisis. And just as a poem by Constantine Cavafy may draw from the past to foresee prospective tragedies "that would later befall Greece" (Argenti 2019: 261), I argue that "prospective memory" of food celebrations such as Easter or the ripening of figs allow people to draw on the past to shape the ordinary future as memorable. In other words, they "prepare in the present for a future memory" (Sutton 2001: 29–31). The analogic thinking discussed above applies as much to everyday meals as to events of capital H History, whereby Kalymnians compare each meal to previous versions of "the same" dish, taking the time to parse the taste of their food. "Proustian" phenomena such as this led me to describe the ways we might think of memory not as a recording device that more or less accurately preserves past events, but as a sense that shapes our experience of the world, just like any of our other culturally honed senses. Memory-as-a-sense can, just as Knight, Stewart, and Argenti suggest, bring something from the distant past into the present in powerful, synesthetic ways:

> A family on the island of Kalymnos watches a show about cooking chickpeas in a clay oven on a neighboring island. This stimulates the wife to identify the chickpea dish as "lemon"-style, not because there is lemon in the recipe but because it didn't have tomato in it as it does on Kalymnos, so it was "white" rather than "red." This got the wife thinking about a trip to another nearby island, Nisyros, where her husband had been working a few years back, and where they cooked chickpeas for one of the local religious festivals. She remembered being struck by the fact that on Nisyros they took basil from their windowsills (basil is decorative, not typically used in Greek cooking), and threw it on the coals where the chickpeas were baking. She describes the striking color of the basil burning on the coals. This leads the son to request chickpeas be made. (Sutton 2011: 471)

In other contexts, chickpeas might be tasted through the filter of wartime memories when they were a starvation food, and thus become a present-day metaphor for austerity.[24]

This is all to say that everyday "histories," or the stories that pass the day in ordinary times, are as much subject to analogic thinking and non-linear tellings as the History that makes up the local and national identities of Kalymnians and other Greeks. These "histories" are also bound up with the attitudes toward risk and dealing with contingency that I described earlier. For to engage with risk, or to "steal a bad hour from death" (Herzfeld 1985), is also to engage with temporality, as Katerina employs a "traditional" can opener that her skill allows her to navigate with danger but without damage. Similarly, she teaches her young granddaughter to fry zucchini slices with a handy spoon that allows for greater control—but once again greater danger—than the safe "modern" implement, the spatula.

As I suggested in the last chapter, much of what makes cooking *cooking* is its inherently risky nature, emphasized in Greece by existential attitudes that celebrate such engagement and have the potential to create memorable meals. The words "to cook" and "to bake" in Greek are also interesting for their metaphorical extensions that suggest both transformation and risk.

Figures 3.7 and 3.8. Katerina Miha frying zucchini and using a knife to cut some of the pieces of zucchini in the pan she had decided were too large to properly brown. © David Sutton.

Mayerevo means "to cook" in the broadest sense, whereas *psino* refers specifically to baking or putting things in an oven (though it can be used for barbeque as well). To say that something is cooking (*kati mayerevetai*), however, suggests a plot or that something suspicious is being developed. "Baking" has even broader associations. A simple "something's baking" (*kati psinetai*) refers to the development of some possibility, such as the beginning of a relationship. Similarly, to "bake someone" means to try to convince them of something in an open way,[25] whereas to cook "a plan," for example, involves some kind of secrecy or alchemy, thus playing on the common understanding of baking as relatively straightforward and rule-bound, whereas cooking can involve many hidden diversions,[26] which may to a much greater extent call on *patendes* in the moment (once you put something in the oven, there is less room for maneuver). Both of these metaphors are built on verbs in the medial-passive voice, suggesting that, in both baking and cooking, one is not fully in control of the process but must persuade recalcitrant humans or material ingredients in order to succeed. Seeing cooking as a metaphor, or model, for social transformation resonates to some degree with Brad Weiss's (1996) work on Haya cooking. Though in the Haya case, these transformations focus on values such as enclosure and dispersal as opposed to what I am describing as a more generalized suggestion of future possibilities, whether suspicious or promising. I think Seremetakis is getting at the same thing when she writes that cooking "is a *poesis*, an act to tactile-affective creation that embodies self-reflexive 'secrets'" (2019: 182). Here she brings together knowledge, emotion, and the senses, all of which, as I have been suggesting in many examples, draw on the past to project possibilities forward on a journey. That journey can reference specific pasts, like the wartime chickpeas, or more general senses of pastness, like Katerina's can opener. Thus, cooking/baking is imagined as a temporal hinge between past and future, binding time or "time-binding," for those willing to risk it.[27]

To think about the future as well as the past also links these ideas about risky cooking in interesting ways. In their work *The Anthropology of the Future*, Rebecca Bryant and Daniel Knight (2019: 175) note their debt to Malaby's work in thinking about the often-ignored issue of contingency, which they argue is a key aspect of approaching the idea of destiny. They draw on the philosophy of David Hume, and in particular the idea of the "secret nature" of things, or the gap between things and their representations, to suggest that the past is a necessary but imperfect guide to the future: "While experience leads to expectation, it also leads to the knowledge that things may turn out differently than we expect" (2019: 169). This does not mean that uncertain destiny leads to passivity, a longtime bugbear of studies of "oriental" societies. On the contrary, it suggests that we must grasp the present both with full knowledge of the past and with a sense of the possibilities for the future (2019: 175).

Possibility and contingency: two words that are very much part of the concept of everyday risk that I have been developing here. But in suggesting that we focus our analysis on the everyday as much as moments of crisis or other focalization points, I fear that I may once again, perhaps, be accused of trivializing. As in chapter 1, I would suggest that the two—crisis and everyday—are tied together, and it is an easy leap (made often by Kalymnians)

between bad neighbors and international politics, just as it is between local food sharing between neighbors and solidarity movements.[28] Cooking
memories, which seem to be about nothing more than the taste of chickpeas,
often act as a way of preserving, in embodied form, oppressed or negated
identities, as noted above. Abarca describes similarly the "palate memory"
for various starches such as sweet potatoes among Latinos, which, she argues, "informs a group's collective sensory memories" even when not con-
sciously recognized by individuals who might claim "[t]here are no Africans
in Cuba," while at other moments recognizing their deep influence on taste
preferences (Abarca 2017: 32–34).[29] As Abarca summarizes, "Through embodied performance, we open the possibility to be able to taste that who we
are today is seasoned with the culinary (ever-changing) inheritance we have
received throughout history" (2017: 36).

Razia Parveen's study of Pakistani diaspora women in a town in West
Yorkshire, UK, focuses on the way local, regional, and national identities
are recreated through the transmission of oral recipes. In a context in which
"authenticity" is highly valued, these recipes transmit the authority of "the
mother's voice" by insisting on repetition with minimal change. They fit,
then, more with Sahlins's description of Maori mythopraxis of following the
models provided by one's (in this case female) ancestors. But also like the
Maori, this allows for not just authentic repetition, but some variation and
autonomy in each instantiation, a negotiation of possibilities in diaspora that
may allow certain tools from the homeland to be replaced by others, and a
certain amount of variation in ingredients—butter or ghee—to allow each
woman the autonomy to navigate between personal and collective memory
while preserving "the mother's voice" (2017: 62). Different levels of identity are reflected in the "specific names of places in the homeland [that] are
mentioned adding to the compartmentalizing of foods and constructing a
cultural identity through ingredients and processes" (2017: 65). Through
what she refers to as "autonetic consciousness," a constant imagining of past
and future in the present, women bridge the distance of migration by reproducing some dishes unchanged, others slightly altered, and others "actively"
forgotten because of their ties to negative past associations (2017: 107).

Thus, in both these cases—the mundane tastes of sweet potatoes or decisions to use butter or ghee—people find expressions of identities, ethnic and
gendered, that might otherwise remain suppressed. And in both instances,
there is a transgression of linear history much like in my Greek examples
above in which moments from the past can suddenly become close, either
through cyclical repetition in Parveen's case or through the surprise of palate
memory for Abarca. In the Kalymnian context, I think about memories of
Italian (colonial) and Turkish influences on Kalymnian taste that challenge
national narratives implicitly and explicitly. One man remembers grilling

eggplant over donkey dung, a potentially embarrassing Turkish influence that was ignored or denied by younger Kalymnians. Others remembered the delicious meats and canned foods brought, and sometimes shared, by the Italian colonists, which they were told not to eat by priests fearing Italian cultural influence on the island (Sutton 2001: 75). There is risk here as well; not quite the risk faced by women who had relationships with Italian soldiers, which could get one killed (Doumanis 1997), but still a willingness to challenge tradition and received ideas in the service of good tastes.

AN AUTOETHNOGRAPHIC INTERLUDE

Sometimes I cook dishes because they call upon some part of my identity or my past, and perhaps you do as well. I have a handful of dishes that I associate with my father, such as the spinach and cheese casserole that was a childhood favorite of mine and I have made perhaps a dozen times since his passing in 1986, a reminder that links both to my memories of him and to the Syrian Jewish heritage that reproduced this food in a new context. I know what my father's acceptable variations were (zucchini was a variation on the dish) and the cheeses he used, perhaps out of convenience in the United States at that time (typically Swiss, and also American Muenster, a cheese that was a staple in the 1970s when it was one of the few available at the supermarket, and one I used to call "monster" cheese, but I have rarely eaten since).[30] Another dish has no Syrian component. In fact, I have no idea how my father decided to first make what he called "Canary Island Pumpkin Soup," which mixed pumpkin with fresh green beans, kidney beans, canned tomatoes, seasonings, and of course a good crusty bread. This became a staple at our table during the mid-1970s and reflected the beginning of incorporating more vegetarian meals in our diet, a growing part of the larger food consciousness in middle-class New York at the time. I have no more clues as to the dish's origin or much else in the hastily scrawled index card that merely lists the key ingredients and some very elliptical instructions. Nor has the internet been much help in this case—surprisingly enough, it is, perhaps, simply one of my father's own "twists." So, while I sometimes come close to reproducing the flavor that I remember, it is almost always a near, or more distant, miss, as so many people report when recreating the recipes of departed grandmothers.

The spinach casserole, thus, evokes my memory of my father, but also my father's memories of his background growing up in a highly religious Syrian-Jewish family with four sisters, in which secular knowledge, except that of specific occupations, was seen to have no value. In this sense he rejected the majority of his past, but preserved some fond memories through cooking, something he was never allowed to do as a child (as the only son with four sisters!). The pumpkin soup, on the other hand, has no connection to the past for my father, and thus for me simply captures a moment in time—well, not a moment, but a period of time, and the many friends with whom we shared meals around our kitchen table when I was growing up in the 1970s. It was a soothing meal—a "good thick soup," as Mary Douglas (1974) describes her proposed substitute for "meat and two veg"—and part of my nascent knowledge of "healthy" vegetarian food. Both of these meals make me think of my father, but with very different histories and different historicities attached. The power of food memories to make the past suddenly close and alive is, of course, the basis of what is referred to as the Proustian phenomenon, a topic that I explored in my earlier work on memory.[31] But this can occur, or be planned for "prospectively," in very different ways with different implications for what one might do with the particular dish and how it might change, develop, or be risked. The spinach casserole is a recipe that I try to keep as close to my memory of its original as possible—like Parveen's Pakistani migrants—in search of that taste that I remember and "my father's voice"; in this regime, even choosing a more interesting cheese than Muenster is not really a consideration. The pumpkin soup, on the other hand, is less weighted by tradition. I have been constantly fiddling around the edges of this recipe, substituting fresh dried beans for canned beans, using my own vegetable stock instead of water, and trying all kinds of things that might make this soup more like itself (partly since the recipe I have is so minimal), but not an exact copy of my father's. This aligns with my sense that he too played with this recipe a bit more than he did with the spinach casserole, where he, too, may have been searching for a flavor from his past. Cookbook author Claudia Roden, with whom I found (over high tea at the School of Oriental and African Studies in London) that I shared an ancestry of Syrian Jewish Rabbis from Aleppo, writes that in cooking, we "summon the ghosts of our past" even as we rejoice in our present (1986: 14).[32] Ghosts are a suggestive metaphor, usually implying unfinished business, or a recognition of more-than-human agency.[33] They suggest to me that the foods that we cook are not more or less risk prone. All foods, in my research on Kalymnos, hum with the possibility of other times and other temporalities, though at different times certain foods, like the chick peas, may be more explicit in their polytemporal possibilities.

But in our present unsettled and unsettling times, we may be increasingly "haunted by the future" as well,[34] especially in a time in which the reality of a global pandemic questions the very possibility of a future that can be seen as "normal." When I wrote my first ethnography of Kalymnos back in the 1990s, I noted that many people in the United States might go along with Francis Fukuyama's famously premature dictum of the "end of history," reflecting a general feeling that history was no longer relevant to the present or that history was "toast."[35] Clearly things have changed. As we live through what is experienced as an increasingly mediated world some suggest has broken our very sense of time,[36] the temporality of cooking and shared meals seems to offer a recognizable salve for our broken experience of the present. But I would suggest here that we think about cooking's temporalities as more risky, full of ghosts of Christmas past and future, as I suggest in my concluding section.

"STRIKING" TEMPORALITIES

For you the food memory trigger might be sight, or taste, or sound, or some sensual mixture of all of it. The point is, we all have recipes we've loved and lost. How serendipitous to rediscover them? Coming around this Lost Recipes corner, I hope you do.

—Monica Rogers, "Lost Recipes Found"

We are free to choose for ourselves not what will become of us, but—once it has come to pass—at what level to create the syntheses of our memories, what moments in time to constitute as an event or as a repetition, and to identify what recursions connect one phase of our lives to another and what occurrences are redolent of what others.

—Nicholas Argenti, *Remembering Absence:*
The Sense of Life in Island Greece

So, I am making the perhaps audacious claim in this chapter that Greek historical consciousness, as explored by a generation of anthropologists, has something to do with the notion of cooking as everyday risk that I've been developing in these pages. Though taking a risk is obviously forward-thinking and forward-sensing,[37] it is also very much in the present, as one seizes the moment and, hopefully, doesn't lose the time invested, but also is very much connected to the past. I am drawn to Walter Benjamin's famous phrase about seizing a memory "as it flashes up in a moment of danger." It resonates with Stavroula Pipyrou's comparison of tricks (*kolpa*) to a "strike" or attack (on ingredients, on a larger context), and to the phrase of Herzfeld's improvising shepherds who hope to "steal a bad hour from death." We are talking about time regained in the Proustian sense, where creating something new, such as an artistic dish or a three-thousand-page novel, requires that one also remains deeply aware of a past of memories and histories that create flavor palates, traditions, robust food cultures,[38] or even cultural structures in Sahlins's sense—transformations that are always also reproductions. While Benjamin (and Argenti) single out moments of danger and crisis respectively, I have been suggesting here that those same processes are at play in the seemingly ordinary moments of life in the kitchens of Greece. Whether it is Katerina and her dangerous, identity-defining can opener, or the many women willing to put themselves in danger, as Pipyrou's friend put it in discussing taking the risk of rolling a pita, these moments are redolent with potentiality: they might become events, for better or worse, or simply help pass the day, with no "histories" in play. And cooking *is cooking*, as I argued in chapter 2, to the extent that it allows for this play of possibility and danger, contingency and imagination.

NOTES

Epigraphs: Athens Chef, cited in Papacharalampous 2019; SBS Radio Cooking Show with Dina Gerolymou, 23 March 2018; Katerina Kardoulia, quoted in Sutton 2014: 63. Section epigraphs: Monica Rogers, "Lost Recipes Found: About." Retrieved 22 April 2021 from http://lostrecipesfound.com/about/; Argenti 2019: 68.

1. This scene is available at David Sutton, "Katerina and the Can Opener," 30 June 2014. Retrieved 22 April 2021 from https://www.youtube.com/watch?v=LQlPycZFS54&feature=emb_logo.
2. This is a concept that Sahlins develops to argue that certain "actors" are structurally in position to have different agency than other actors. His later work, *Apologies to Thucydides* (2004), is essentially an extended argument on this point, drawing on examples ranging from the Peloponnesian Wars to the 1951 baseball season.
3. Graham Jones's study of street magicians in Paris also stresses this performative element in which the precondition for satisfactory magical performance is that it be risky (Jones 2011: 9).
4. On the sponge diving industry in Kalymnos, see Bernard 1976. For a thoughtful questioning of the willingness of men to risk their lives in sponge diving, see Kalafatas 2003.
5. See Salamone and Stanton (1986) and du Boulay and Williams (1987) on the importance of the housewife and making do with what was available as an affirmation of family reputation.
6. In Kalymnos, I heard such dishes sometimes referred to as "prostitute" food because they suggested the possibility that you were in a hurry to finish cooking so that you had time for illicit assignations.
7. Pipyrou, personal communication with author via Skype, 25 January 2020.
8. A point that Harry West (2020) makes for preserving "tradition" in contemporary cheesemaking in the context of often embracing new technologies.
9. Thanks to Nafsika Papacharalampous for alerting me to these *kolpa*.
10. The Greek website "Golden Recipes" offers the "trick" of covering beef filets with coarse salt for several hours before cooking as a way to tenderize tough meat or simply make any quality of filet "melt in your mouth." "Make the Meat Melt in Your Mouth! This Is the Very Easy 'Trick' that Few Know!" *Golden Recipes*, 4 February 2018. Retrieved 22 April 2021 from https://www.xrysessyntages.gr/κάντε-το-

κρέας-να-λιώνει-στο-στόμα-αυτό/?fbclid=IwAR0ebWYxLw0jEeXbiAtv9sUy
t5LVr48uidxAf399Gvpna28Xj_2lmUcWwwE

11. On one occasion I also heard the Greek word "combines" or "swindles" used to talk about cooking tricks, which seemed to suggest "putting one over" on people, perhaps by finding ways to make an old rind of cheese usable by gently steaming it over a pot of cooking food.

12. Leo Vournelis, personal communication, 2 November 2019.

13. Neni Panourgia, personal communication, 30 October 2019.

14. Stavroula Pipyrou, personal communication, 25 January 2020.

15. These are very different from the now ubiquitous cooking "hacks" in the United States, which are often promulgated in YouTube videos, such as better ways to peel garlic or remove the pit from an avocado. In her study of digital food, Tania Lewis notes that hacks usually involve "finding an ingenious, simple way to make everyday food preparation and cookery quicker and more efficient" (Lewis 2020: 63). In this sense it is different from tricks and patents in its focus on efficiency rather than socially embedded taste. It is more, perhaps, like a grassroots culinary perfectionism as discussed in the last chapter, the "best" way to cut an onion, etc. How internet cooking hacks are actually invented and put into practice in the United States (and elsewhere!) awaits ethnographic exploration.

16. Nafsika Papaharalampous conveyed this quote to me from her mother Katerina, 4 December 2020.

17. The etymology of the word *mistiko* comes from the word miïsi, (pronounced MEE-EESEE) or initiation, as into mysteries, once again implying something not readily available.

18. See Sutton 2014: 119–21 for the full context of this example.

19. *Mastoras* is also a term used typically for an older, retired man out of respect and recognition of his life-long labor. This can be used even if the man's occupation was not a craft per se, as I heard older shepherds on Kalymnos referred to as *mastoras*.

20. See Sutton 2001: chap. 3, 2014: chap. 1.

21. Thanks to Renee Hirschon for this observation.

22. Argenti 2019; Hamilakis 2014; Knight 2015; Stewart 2012.

23. Stewart and Palmié 2016; Hamilakis 2008.

24. On chickpeas and wartime starvation, see Panourgia 2009: 64. On chickpeas and austerity, see Sutton 2016b.

25. You can bake someone to convince them to go to a movie, or you can bake a lover to get her or him into bed, but in each case, it is a relatively straightforward matter, dependent on your verbal skill. I am grateful to Leo Vournelis for clarifying some of these metaphorical meanings.

26. Of course, baking also involves all kinds of tacit knowledge, as Amy Trubek (2017) argues in her discussion of the craft of wild yeast bread baking.

27. As James Fernandez discusses one of the key aspects of metaphor in his analysis of a Bwiti sermon in Gabon: "In respect to our sermon, what is being said is not only that the present has something very pastlike, but the past has something very present-like. In the transitional period, with its painful dichotomy between past and present, a sermon that can make a unity of these two diverse periods cannot fail to appeal. It has accomplished what is after all one of the chief contributions of culture—*time-binding*" (1966: 69, my emphasis).

28. See Sutton 2021.

29. The same man who denies African presence in Cuba notes multiple African influences on his own palate memory: "'Every time an African did something, he did it well. He brought the recipe from his land, from Africa. Of the things I liked . . . the best were the fritters" (Abarca 2017: 33).

30. Some recipes on the internet call for feta cheese as well as parmesan, which in the abstract sound appealing, but the feta, of course, would bring it too close to a Greek dish, which is in this case very much not what I am going for and would certainly interfere with the memory process.

31. Sutton 2001: chap. 3.

32. On Greek history itself as a "ghostly presence," see Yalouri 2014: 167.

33. As in Daniel Miller's discussion of haunted houses (2010: 93–94).

34. See discussion in Albro 2019.

35. Sutton 1998: 210.

36. See Katherine Miller, "The 2010s Broke Our Sense of Time," *Buzzfeed News*, 24 October 2019. Retrieved 22 April 2021 from https://www.buzzfeednews.com/article/katherinemiller/the-2010s-have-broken-our-sense-of-time. I quote Miller at length because I like this quote:

    This is why algorithmic time is so disorienting and why it bends your mind. Everything good, bad, and complicated flows through our phones, and for those not living some hippie Walden trip, we operate inside a technological experience that moves forward and back, and pulls you with it. Using a phone is tied up with the relentless, perpendicular feeling of living through the Trump presidency: the algorithms that are never quite with you in the moment, the imperishable supply of new Instagram stories, the scrolling through what you said six hours ago, the four new texts, the absence of texts, that text from three days ago that has warmed up your entire life, the four versions of the same news alert. You can find yourself wondering why you're seeing this now—or knowing too well why it is so. You can feel amazing and awful—exult in and be repelled by life—in the space of seconds. The thing you must say, the thing you've been waiting for—it's always there, pulling you back under again and again and again. Who can remember anything anymore?

    This was written before the coronavirus, which has perhaps made these habits even more compulsive.

37. As discussed in chapter 2.

38. See Sutton 2016b.

TAKE THE RISK

> Embracing uncertainty involves acknowledging that we do not and cannot know exactly what will happen next, and engaging with the possibilities that this affords.
>
> —Yoko Akama, Sarah Pink, and Shanti
> Sumartojo, *Uncertainty and Possibility*

In the closing days of the second decade of the twenty-first century, recipes were in the headlines. It seems that the white nationalists of Italy's far-right Italian League had found another cause for outrage in the Vatican's decision to serve a "meal for the poor," including lasagna made with beef rather than pork, to better serve Muslim (and Jewish) guests. One right-wing commentator responded to this act of sensitivity by accusing the Pope of subscribing to "a suicidal, multiculturalist ideology that leads to the rejection of all that is Christian or Western."[1] This conflict reminds me of accounts of other dishes at other times, such as early twentieth-century America, when Italians were in fact the "other," and garlic and even tomato sauce were deemed un-American ingredients and demands were made to remove them from a proper and healthy diet.[2] I am also reminded of accounts of changes in ingredients embarked on willingly, such as Steve Yarbrough's remembrance of his Mississippi grandmother's eschewing of hush puppies, fried catfish, and other delicacies of his childhood in favor of Wonder bread and Kraft macaroni and cheese, choices that, when challenged, she defended vigorously: "This ain't the days of covered wagons. This is the modern world. And I for one refuse to regret it" (Yarbrough 2001: 219). At the same time, food writer Mai Tran decries the "purists and food zealots" who insist on authenticity of both ingredients and chefs' identities, policing restaurants purveying "new" cuisines in the US scene such as Vietnamese. As she notes, "recipes aren't stagnant, and neither is culture. Vestiges of French colonization are abundant in Vietnamese food, from Café du Monde coffee to bành mì baguettes, but these are now considered inherently Vietnamese, even as we distance ourselves from an imperialist past."[3] These examples clearly show how a shift in ingredients, small or large, can index much larger questions of identities, gender relations, politics, and shifting societal understandings of sensory experience, and that these changes and continuities are risky in the multiple ways that I have been exploring. Of course, not all ingredients are so iconic or momentous. They may, like those I documented for moussaka in Greece, reflect simply small shifts and twists that occur in the span of the life of a family or community. And yet, they can still be analytically revealing as they speak to the process of cooking that calls on the traditional, the "of the moment," and/or the forward thinking. Choices of ingredients disclose processes and practices of comfort and familiarity, desire and aspiration, boredom and creativity, and shallow or deep histories.

I think of a pasta dish with peanut butter, tamari sauce, vinegar (ideally rice, but apple cider is really okay), garlic, and scallions. I found it in what was, in the mid-1980s, my go-to cookbook: *Jane Brody's Good Food Book* (1985). Since then, I have made this recipe several hundred times, both for myself, my family, and company. But adapted it as well: a bit more vinegar, a bit more peanut butter, fewer red-pepper flakes for my children, and more hot pepper of whatever type I had on hand for myself. While I was not a vegetarian when I first made it, it became part of my vegetarian fare, and at times a staple for its simplicity and easiness to prepare (only twenty minutes or so). Over time I added more ingredients to make it seem like more of a one-pot meal; mushrooms ideally, sometimes sweet bell peppers, sometimes even broccoli or greens of some kind, though the latter seemed less successful. Sometimes I added a meat substitute like Quorn or tofu, to mimic the way I have seen sesame noodles prepared with a bit of ground meat. Some of these modifications were when I made it for guests, although it was a dish that frustrated me in bringing it to a party potluck, because it demands extra tamari sauce to be sprinkled on top just before consuming, an instruction that one simply cannot convey in the context of a potluck. At a certain point concerns over sodium led me to substitute low-sodium tamari for regular. In more recent years, orders of sesame noodles from Chinese restaurants inspired me to try adding strings of cucumber to the dish, with mixed results. This was the one dish that I passed on to my elder son, and it became his go-to dish, one of the few actual dishes that he could cook, when he went away to college. He, however, stopped eating it after about five years of making it for himself when he decided to cut carbs from his diet, though recently has sought the same flavor with an order of Peanut Chicken from our local Chinese take-out.

And I find myself, on the cusp of 2020, wondering why I have rarely made it in the past two years. Boredom, or perhaps concern that, despite Jane Brody, all those carbs really are not so healthy after all? This is not like other dishes that I cook specifically because they remind me of people from my past: my father's Syrian spinach casserole or his so-called "Canary Island Pumpkin Soup," which I had not had for nearly thirty years when I rediscovered it. There was the version of lo mein that my beloved Aunt Edith used to make for me almost every time I visited her from the early 1980s to her death in the late 1990s, and I have made it regularly since then. Or the grapefruit and avocado salad with blue cheese dressing, which I learned as a teenager from my upstairs neighbor, Ruth Hamlin, nearly forty years ago. As a retired music teacher, she had taken an interest in, and wished to encourage, my cooking imagination. This dish became my wife's favorite, always requested for her birthday or other occasions. These tastes are specifically Proustian in that cooking and eating them is meant to evoke memories of those departed figures, even if I have altered some of the recipes because of forgetfulness or the desire to change certain things (substituting a better quality soy sauce in the lo mein dish for the La Choy brand my aunt swore by), while others have remained more resistant to change: the salad, because of its simplicity, is the same three ingredients (not counting the dressing) that it always was, despite occasional attempts to add radicchio and pomegranate seeds or to substitute oranges for grapefruit when my mother had excised that ingredient from her diet.

The insights provided by this brief autoethnography are, once again, revealing in small ways. But I would suggest that they are responsive to the kind of approaches to change and continuity that I have laid out in these pages. Mary Douglas has suggested metaphorically that the cycle of meals over the course of a lifetime, like the daily, weekly, and yearly cycles, might not only parallel each other, but provide a structure that reflects the "grand pattern" of a life (1982: 116). But while meal patterns have been recorded by many food scholars, the slow mutations of dishes and the changing ways that we cook them has never received ethnographic attention. Treating such as data—which might tell us about both everyday practice and its relationship to questions of how we experience the relation of tradition and creativity, past, present, and future—is the wager I have made on an approach that sees cooking as a daily risky endeavor. It is part of a critique of approaches that associate tradition with stereotypical reproduction, while reserving creativity for the modern individual of typically Western origins. In criticizing the modernist view of creativity versus traditionalism, Bruner notes that all people "construct culture as they go along and as they respond to life's contingencies" (Bruner, cited in Hallam and Ingold 2007: 2). All people, "traditional" and "modern" alike, are constantly improvising because "no system of codes, rules and norms can anticipate every possible circumstance" (Hallam and Ingold 2007: 2), or as Sahlins would say, categories are "a great gamble played with the empirical realities" (1985: 149). This holds true even if, as argued in chapter 3, different cultures may have different ways of talking about risk, continuity, and change. Given this understanding, I would argue that it is as important to study contingency, risk, and creativity in the everyday kitchens of ordinary toiling cooks as it is to study those of molecular gastronomists and other famed chefs de jour.

Accepting the risk of cooking might strike a change in the culture of culinary perfectionism, or "fascism" according to Finn, at a time when fascism seems to be creeping into more and more aspects of contemporary life. The embrace of contingency as an existential aspect of a collective life, which can only lead one to hope for "good continuity," suggests one antidote to a culture that bounces between submission to authorities and to external, decontextualized knowledge and rules—Lorraine Daston's (2019) "delusion of the perfect rule"—and a rejection of all collective projects and goals in the service of the pursuit of neoliberal individualization of risks and rewards. Tricks and patents do not mean a rejection of order or rules tout court, and an embrace of the stereotyped Eastern trickster. Rather, they are about recognizing the multiple twists and turns—some more successful than others— that gets one to their destination. They entail retaining a sense of agency even as one recognizes the importance of collective negotiations of risk and responsibility, and collective judgments of the taste of recognized recipes and dishes.

Finn, indeed, points us to alternatives to culinary perfectionism, such as the "improvisational" cooking of Sally Schneider (2006). Schneider, like Finn, identifies perfectionism as the enemy of her approach and notes that "improvisation runs counter to any sort of codification: it springs out of a moment in a process that remains, mostly, mysterious" (2006: 3). Indeed, Schneider wants to balance the knowledge of process with that sense of mystery and discovery, that allows for a "cascade" of recipes, through improvisation and "see[ing] what happens" (2006: 4). This is an idea that we can find echoed in other current writings, such as Priya Basil's thoughts on food and hospitality, in which she notes "Recipes are the original open source, offering building blocks that may be adjusted across time, place and seasons to create infinite dishes" (2019: 13). In a *New York Times* recipe for hash browns by Sam Sifton (2016), Sifton notes that the recipe was taken from a wonderful breakfast that he had while on vacation on San Juan Island, and he started making it when he returned home. But because it was complicated, and his kids wanted to eat it all the time, he developed a hack which made the recipe "something else again." As he describes it, he cubed the potatoes instead of grating them and roasted them rather than frying them in clarified butter, among other adaptations. He concludes, "It looks nothing like what I ate on San Juan, and its flavor outstrips my memory of the original." This leads him to reflect, "Recipes change over time, if you make them enough. Recipes change in response to experience at the stove and, if you're lucky, because of experiences you have out in the world, eating and thinking" (Sifton 2016: 27). Both at the stove and in the world: a good metaphor for the bi-directionality of any good analysis of cooking.

Mark Bittman's recent cookbook *Dinner for Everyone* (2019), similarly features three versions of each recipe: one for company, one for every day, and one vegetarian version. On the *Slate Culture Gabfest*, Julia Turner reflects on Bittman's inspiration, noting that she took his sardine pasta recipe and ran with it, changing the proportions. She claims, "I doubled the parsley, tripled the lemon, added hot pepper flakes so that has some kick to it . . . I have my own version of it now that's distinct enough from his and his ratios that it's probably now its own recipe, but he's the person who gave me the idea of doing that with the sardines on the back shelf of my cabinet."[4] This is echoed more generally by Sally Schneider's suggestion that we take from other cooks, "extracting a kernel of an idea or a combination of flavorings or a technique to use in [one's] own improvisations" (2006: 13).

In this process Schneider suggests overcoming the fear of "listening to your senses" and expressing your culinary "voice," a metaphor that many have found useful in thinking in particular about the significance of women's kitchen activities in building identities and resistances (Counihan 2004; Hauck-Lawson 1998).[5] If this sounds very much like the "skill" and sensory attentiveness that I discussed in chapter 2 in relation to David Pye's and Tim Ingold's theories, Schneider also sees inspiration that might lead one to take chances in the kitchen in polytemporal terms, very much in line with the historical consciousness I describe in chapter 3. She notes that inspiration is not a linear process, but a "zigzagging flux of ideas, memories, snipped of recipes and hungers . . . largely a process of association" (2006: 13), which notably combines past (memories), present ("what's in front of you in your field of vision"), and future ("hungers," i.e., desires). Most of all, she insists that you embrace the unexpected: "Often this means you start out with one thing in mind but, as you cook, the idea shifts and evolves until you find yourself on a different path than the one you started" (2006: 9). This process echoes the kind of shift of categories that Sahlins has given us as a model for understanding change, noting that accidents often bring delicious results.

But changes can still provoke outrage as well. Especially when recipes enter the public domain, more seems to be at stake. As announced by the headline in *The Guardian* "Stop This Madness," recounting the response to a

New York Times recipe for "Smoky Tomato Carbonara,"[6] which, in the par-
lance of our times, blew up on social media as noted Italian chefs and other
guardians of culture expressed their dismay at the notion that a carbonara
recipe could include tomatoes. One Rome-based chef excoriated the *New
York Times* in language that perfectly tracks with my discussion of moussaka
inventions: "It would be like putting salami in a cappuccino or mortadella
in sushi. OK, fine, but then let's not call it sushi, similarly with this one—
carbonara with tomato is not carbonara. It's something else." While a statement from the Italian Farmers Association emphasized "the real risk" of this
was that a "fake" or "falsified" dish would become associated internationally
with "authentic" Italian tradition, thus changing the dish too quickly not just
for one family or one community but for the wider world for whom Italian
food is a brand in need of protection. However, as I have been suggesting
throughout, this process can be reproduced at the level of small community
(Kalymnos) or even family, though perhaps with less vitriol given that the
careers of chefs and commodities are not typically at stake. Once again, this
example stresses the larger identities that can be put at risk in small decisions
to reproduce or change a recipe.

The examples here culled from various sources of popular culture, like
those discussed throughout based on my fieldwork in Greece, are hardly
meant to be conclusive or definitive answers to the question "what is cooking"? My approach to cooking as everyday risk, as I have presented it here, is
primarily meant to be suggestive of a methodology that might be revelatory
for a comparative anthropological understanding of cooking and everyday
life. Ever since the fieldwork of Audrey Richards (1939) and Rosemary Firth
(1966) in the early to mid-twentieth century, anthropologists have known
that studying everyday cooking can be a revealing part of our ethnographic
toolkit, raising issues of power, knowledge, time, household structure, and
reproduction. And yet, despite these promising beginnings, cooking remains among the most neglected topics in the study of everyday life, largely
because it was long overlooked as insignificant, female labor. In this book
I have suggested not just that cooking needs to be studied because it has
been ignored, but because it provides us a way to answer questions about
tradition and change, or continuity and innovation, that have implications
for our anthropology more broadly. Nir Avieli suggests that the power of
food symbolism comes from the fact that food, unlike other material culture,
is constantly transforming—through cooking, eating, and digesting: "It is
the elasticity of the means that allows the elasticity of meanings."[7] Indeed,
I agree, but suggest here further that food's constant transformations allow
us to track those meanings in real time. This will give us a window into how
people think about continuity and change and practice those intuitions.

A recent review of studies of "events" in anthropology notes the difficulty of anthropologists planning research around being there when the events "happen" (Van Dooremalen 2017). With cooking, however, I have argued that the definition of "event" and "happening" allows us to think through questions of how both change and continuity take work in the sense of interpretive work on the part of our subjects and ourselves. Extant studies of cooking in food studies more broadly may document certain changes in cooking practices—such as shifts in cooking tools, technologies, or ingredients over time—but do little to get at the sense of how the changes and continuities documented are experienced "on the ground" or in the kitchens of countless, mostly female, cooks. But to get at practice—to get at the everyday—we need a method that actually studies practice in its everyday-ness, in the repeated acts that both reproduce and change those practices in each instantiation. In the same way, and despite the work of David Howes (2003) and others to establish the Anthropology of the Senses as a thriving subfield, we have very few studies of everyday tasting. What few studies that exist tend to be of tasting events that are marked out as special rather than tasting as it happens in daily life and in relation to other sensory experiences.[8] We need anthropological studies of cooking that are now missing from the ethnographic record. In invoking the ethnographic record, I am, of course, not suggesting that these studies should be untheorized, and I have attempted to offer one theory in these pages (no doubt others will emerge with further ethnography). But I have little doubt that whether confirming or contradicting the idea of everyday risk, a kitchen-based ethnography that follows the repeated daily practice of minute reproductions and transformations, drudgery and imagination, will open up considerable new insights and challenging perspectives. It will provide us, indeed, with bigger fish to fry, and make good on the old promise that cooking is truly good to think.

CODA

As I was revising this manuscript, the world entered the age of COVID-19. From the point of view of several months into the pandemic, cooking is clearly one terrain in which "the new normal" is being played out. In the United States, underpaid "essential workers" in the meat industry were quickly forced back to work by their employers and by presidential order, with predictable tolls on their health, but in the service of not revisiting or bringing change to the American diet, whatever the cost (Pollan 2020). Here risk plays out on the grand scale, the "risk society" imagined by Ulrich Beck, experienced unequally through race, class, and citizenship, in the service of returning to a calming sense of normality for some, no matter the cost in lives. In Greece, on the other hand, despite the threats of social distancing to the fabric of Greek daily life, the majority of people cooperated with government measures. Not because they suddenly developed a fear of everyday risk or the contingencies of life, but because they seemed to use their well-developed sense of contingency to acknowledge that lockdown was safer than putting their fates in the hands of a Greek medical system shredded by years of austerity. In other words, collective responsibility and responsibility for the collective is not the same as some abstract idea of "trust in government" as much anthropology has shown.[9] And while some debated church functioning during the lockdown (Kalantzis 2020) and whether the blessings of Holy Water and Communion Bread provided protection from viruses, the vast majority of Greeks were satisfied with what is in fact a traditional practice of broadcasting liturgies over the airwaves or over loudspeakers as fulfillment of religious obligations. On Kalymnos, and presumably elsewhere in Greece, everyday practices of maintaining community such as regular sharing of food with neighbors (Sutton 2021) were put on hold for a larger sense of collective good, while in the United States many loudly decried the indignity of wearing masks as an attack on their individual rights. Once again, this points to the fact that the relationship between everyday practices of contingency and larger ideologies is itself contingent, unpredictable, and worthy of future research amid all of the massive research that will no doubt be devoted to understanding COVID-19's impact.

In terms of daily food practices, after the early days and the fading of the Toilet Paper Panic, new items seemed to be disappearing from supermarket shelves in the United States. These included yeast, flour, and the sad bags of dried beans that never seemed to sell in pre-pandemic times, potentially indicating a renaissance in cooking, perhaps offset by the runs on frozen pizzas, macaroni and cheese, and Hamburger Helper. As one article noted, people are eating nostalgically: "Consumers are reaching for foods that trigger a comforting childhood memory or are simply their go-to snack when they need to relieve stress," which is bringing forth many childhood food memories.[10] While some of these involved items like "Kraft Easy Cheese" (a variation on Cheez Whiz), who knows what forgotten childhood recipes might be accessed, as many—at least those middle-class non-essential workers sheltering in place—suddenly found themselves with time to cook. As Jesse Dart found in interviewing sixty-one Italian and Italian-American residents of locked-down Northern Italy, many reported either a discovery or an extension of what people were calling experimentation in the kitchen. One typical response was: "Yes absolutely. I am trying out new recipes online or ones I had saved from a while ago as well as just making things I know. Definitely felt like a good time to use cooking as a way to fill time." Another respondent noted: "I'm always experimenting, even in normal times. It's a creative outlet and now I appreciate it more than ever."[11] From Greece, I find that a close friend, Katerina Miha,[12] who is in her late twenties, and usually busy with her budding career in beauty and fashion in Athens, has used lockdown time at home to learn to make bread for the first time from a friend (the first time she went out). She notes that she kneaded it herself, the process was easy, and it gave her the opportunity to see that she could make her own bread for the next time she is not able to go to the baker. She fills her Instagram feed with videos of her making stuffed grape leaves, pictures of various fish dishes and, of course, the freshly baked bread. She told me that she made fish when she returned to Athens (still under lockdown), and was missing Kalymnos and her father's freshly caught fish.

Throughout the United States and Europe, perhaps one of the biggest early pandemic trends (with a massive Instagram presence) was the growth of bread-baking. Particularly striking were the sourdough starters, which can take at least a week to form—not your usual thirty-minute meal![13] While baking in general seems to fit into the category of comfort food, some suggested that there was something particularly satisfying about working dough as an anti-stress activity. But food historian Jane Ziegelman noted other knock-on effects of bread-baking in her talk on Great Depression eating, which involved many comparisons with the present. As she put it, "learning how to bake bread [is] learning how to make substitutions, and that involves learning food dynamics."[14] Food blogger Mandy Lee, interviewed on the podcast *The Sporkful with Dan Pashman* discussing her book on "Escapist Cooking" (2019), develops this idea further. She claims that bread-baking is particularly appropriate as escapist cooking because of its contingency:

> I think it's because bread is completely unpredictable. And I think bread is a good place to start because you don't want something that's reliable. Because then that draws you to ask questions. Why did it turn out better last time than this time, what did I do different, was it the moisture in the air, was it the temperature? Was the hand feel of the dough feels different [sic], it sort of invites you to be curious.[15]

Risky cooking indeed! One barely needs to emphasize the contrast with the predictability and removal of human hands and judgment in "no-time" methods of industrial bread production. And the addition of sourdough to the mix, with its unpredictable starter, makes for all the more contingent and crafty outcomes, also displayed with pride in Instagram feeds in the first several months of the pandemic. Andrea Schweitzer-Gil (2020) analyzes these Instagram feeds, noting the power of these pictures to "excite feelings of intimacy by making shared food consumption imaginable even across distance." Schweitzer-Gil also underlines Lee's point in describing the challenge of sourdough starter, concluding: "The discipline required to make sourdough

Figure 4.1. Sourdough bread iteration 47. Photo courtesy of Samuel Rowe-Sutton.

bread can be a welcome routine during this time of uncertainty" (2020), thereby nicely bringing together the "bad" risk of COVID-19 uncertainty and Beck's risk society with the kind of productive risk that I have been discussing throughout this book.[16] She also suggests some of the larger field of references that sourdough offers bakers: "Sharing the process of sourdough baking through social media allows some cooks to engage with an imagined traditional past when our ancestors were more involved in the process of food production. Perhaps things were simpler then, or maybe the idea of an uncertain future was less disconcerting" (Schweitzer-Gil 2020). At the same time, others were taking the meme of bread-baking in a different direction, as in a much-circulated article "Fuck the Bread, The Bread is Over," in which the author uses it as a metonym for neoliberal (female) overachievement and the skewed values of pre-COVID-19 times.[17]

My wife Beth, a long-time baker, took the opportunity to make her first sourdough starter as well. The starter survived the summer, and by December we estimated that it had produced about fifty delicious loaves. However, this was not without debate. On about her fourth loaf, Beth noted that it did not rise as much as before, or have the same delicious, chewy, vaguely caramel-y, and slightly burnt flavor on the crust. She speculated that it was a change in the brand of flour or perhaps our oven's unreliability that led to this divergent outcome.

This recalled to mind what my colleague Leo Vournelis told me about his grandmother, who would make the sign of a cross in the air over the oven each time she put a loaf in to bake, recognizing that her own bodily ability to manage contingency stopped at the closing of the oven door; the rest was up to divine intervention.

Schweitzer-Gil, however, brings it back to memory, describing the sourdough bread as displaying the hum of polytemporality that I discussed in the previous chapter. Indeed, anything fermented is literally made up of many different organisms at different stages in their life process, suggesting another polytemporal metaphor. For Schweitzer-Gil, however, all cooking during the pandemic has become about temporal orientations to the past and to the future. As she puts it: "I have spent more time experimenting with recipes that remind me of my childhood,"[18] while she imagines making these dishes for friends on their post-lockdown reunions. Once again we see how dealing with contingency bridges everyday practices of navigating cooking, and more existential questions about identity, memory, and temporality. While many ethnographic questions remain in the offing, the convergence of cooking and risk will no doubt remain as trenchant After COVID as they were Before COVID.

NOTES

Epigraph: Akama, Pink, and Sumartojo 2018: 36.

1. Giorgio Ghiglione, "Pope Francis's Heretical Pasta," *Foreign Policy*, 24 December 2019. Retrieved 1 December 2020 from https://foreignpolicy.com/2019/12/24/pope-franciss-heretical-pasta/?fbclid=IwAR1X6bO0k-4ZxXeFknbyI5PUVG4yC_xdgUHbo-D0nZ7ODicfrhQYIp7dip0.
2. See Gabaccia 1998, and for a beautiful personal account, Girardi 2001.
3. Mai Tran, "Ignore the Purists and Food Zealots: There Is No Such Thing as 'Authentic' Cuisine," *The Guardian*, 1 January 2020. Retrieved 1 December 2020 from https://www.theguardian.com/commentisfree/2020/jan/01/no-such-thing-authentic-cuisine-vietnamese-food-politics.
4. Culture Gabfest, week of 13 February 2019.
5. Meanwhile, the world of commodified cooking products is always coming up with new ways to bypass the senses. As I was writing this, the gourmet website *Food52* came out with an "adjustable" rolling pin with rings of different depths that you can add to each end in order to guarantee the thickness of the dough. The promotion promises that for just $39, you can "say goodbye to guesswork." I shudder to think what Kalymnians would say about this. "Five Two Adjustable Rolling Pin," *Food52*. Retrieved 1 December 2020 from https://food52.com/shop/products/7635-five-two-adjustable-teak-rolling-pin.
6. Angela Giuffrida, "'Stop This Madness': NYT Angers Italians with 'Smoky Tomato Carbonara' recipe," *The Guardian*, 25 February 2021. Retrieved 25 February 2021 from https://www.theguardian.com/food/2021/feb/25/stop-this-madness-nyt-angers-italians-with-smoky-tomato-carbonara-recipe.

7. This as part of an argument about the power of the symbolism of hummus in the recent "hummus wars" over the dish's disputed origins (Avieli 2016: 53).

8. Excellent studies of tasting events include those of Susan Terrio (2000), Carole Counihan (2018) and Christy Shields-Argeles (2018). The one study I know of that attempts to focus on tasting as everyday practice is Anna Mann's (2015) thesis on "mundane tasting," though here, too, the analysis focuses on a few particular events rather than the daily, repeated practice of tasting.

9. See Sutton 2003; Theodossopoulos 2014.

10. Julie Creswell, "'I Just Need the Comfort': Processed Foods Make a Pandemic Comeback," *The New York Times,* 7 April 2020. Retrieved 1 December 2020 from https://www.nytimes.com/2020/04/07/business/coronavirus-processed-foods.html?fbclid=IwAR1P5mNgTWWtNhOv8aHvZCFpR35icBasC_7gUwRJ4E5HU-cQJVsXP1qNEHc. Other articles also seem to conclude that the pandemic is reinforcing the importance of convenience for typical US households. As one article, citing the rise in food delivery and other conveniences during the pandemic, claimed: "When it is all said and done, the real change brought about by the coronavirus won't be a back-to-the-kitchen movement. It will be a rush toward hyper-convenience at mealtime that could make us more reliant than ever on food prepared by other people." Jane Black and Brent Cunningham, "The Pandemic Is Changing How We Eat: But Not for the Better," *The Washington Post,* 8 May 2020. Retrieved 1 December 2020 from https://www.washingtonpost.com/outlook/the-pandemic-is-changing-how-we-eat-but-not-for-the-better/2020/05/07/5e4623e6-906b-11ea-a9c0-73b93422d691_story.html?fbclid=IwAR2rgEMERmYYBu7Qzbv2N8GZRbKEelgrhW0_G744rJVBRk4KNgoeD4Wak9c.

11. Jesse Dart, unpublished manuscript shared with author.

12. Granddaughter of Katerina Kardoulia of my can opener discussion in chapter 3.

13. Jane Sponagle, "Sourdough Baking Sees Rise in Popularity during COVID-19 Pandemic," *CBC,* 12 April 2020. Retrieved 1 December 2020 from https://www.cbc.ca/news/canada/north/sourdough-popular-covid-19-1.5529649.

14. Tenement Museum, "Virtual Book Talk: A Square Meal," 6 May 2020. Retrieved 5 May 2020 from https://www.youtube.com/watch?v=B1uUcYdMi5s. A spate of Youtube videos also offered Great Depression recipe ideas like Dandelion Salad, presented by a 94-year-old survivor of the Great Depression. See Great Depression Cooking, "Great Depression Cooking—Dandelion Salad," 15 August 2009. Retrieved 5 May 2020 from https://www.youtube.com/watch?v=51VhG8MKxJY.

15. Andres O'Hara, "What's with All The Broken Dishes?" *The Sporkful with Dan Pashman,* 27 April 2020, 6:10–5:27 remaining. Retrieved 1 December 2020 from http://www.sporkful.com/whats-with-all-broken-dishes/.

16. For a consideration of the productivity of uncertainty in thinking about the Greek Crisis, see Yalouri 2018.

17. Sabrina Orah Mark, "Fuck the Bread: The Bread Is Over," *The Paris Review,* 7 May 2020. Retrieved 1 December 2020 from https://www.theparisreview.org/blog/2020/05/07/fuck-the-bread-the-bread-is-over/. The question of how much lockdown cooking is being done by women also demands ethnographic attention. A study of "housework" suggests considerable imbalances, without, however, specifying cooking as a particular category of housework. See Claire Caine Miller, "Nearly Half of Men Say They Do Most of the Home Schooling: 3 Percent of Women Agree,"

The New York Times, 6 May 2020. Retrieved 1 December 2020 from https://www
.nytimes.com/2020/05/06/upshot/pandemic-chores-homeschooling-gender.html.

18. Many COVID food articles stressed this. See, e.g., Maggie Hennessey's "My
Time-Traveling Bowl of Spaghetti and Meat Sauce" in which she writes: "now that
a pandemic has largely confined me within the walls of my Chicago apartment,
with nary a dinner reservation or far-flung trip on the horizon, meat sauce, in its
endless comfy guises, carries a weightier load—of transporting me somewhere else
until I reach the bottom of the bowl." Maggie Hennessy, "My Time-Traveling Bowl
of Spaghetti and Meat Sauce," *Food52,* 17 July 2020. Retrieved 1 December 2020
from   https://food52.com/blog/25435-how-spaghetti-meat-sauce-helps-me-time-
travel/. Interestingly for my purposes, the article explores how Hennessey can make
many variations on the base tomato sauce, depending on whether she wants to imagine traveling in space to other places (New Orleans, Bologna) or in time back to her
mother's table.

REFERENCES

Abarca, Meredith. 2006. *Voices in the Kitchen: Views of Food and the World from Working-Class Mexican and Mexican-American Women*. College Station: Texas A&M Press.
———. 2017. "Afro-Latina/os' Culinary Subjectivities: Rooting Ethnicities through Root Vegetables." In *Food across Borders*, ed. Matt Garcia, E. Melanie DuPuis, and Don Mitchell, 24–43. New Brunswick, NJ: Rutgers University Press.
Adamson, Glenn. 2013. *Thinking through Craft*. Oxford: Berg.
Adapon, Joy. 2008 *Culinary Art and Anthropology*. Oxford: Berg.
Akama, Yoko, Sarah Pink, and Shanti Sumartojo. 2018. *Uncertainty and Possibility: New Approaches to Future Making in Design Anthropology*. London: Bloomsbury.
Albro, Robert. 2019. "From Cultures to Ontologies to Hauntologies and States of Interpretive Puzzlement in Anthropology." Paper presented at AAA Annual Meetings, Vancouver, BC, November 22.
Appadurai, Arjun. 2012. "The Spirit of Calculation." *Cambridge Anthropology* 30(1): 3–17.
Argenti, Nicholas. 2019. *Remembering Absence: The Sense of Life in Island Greece*. Bloomington: Indiana University Press.
Arnoldi, Jakob. 2009. *Risk*. London: Polity.
Avieli, Nir. 2016. "The Hummus Wars: Local Food, Guinness Records and Palestinian-Israeli Gastropolitics." In *Cooking Cultures: Convergent Histories of Food and Feeling*, ed. Ishita Banerjee-Dube, 39–57. Cambridge: Cambridge University Press.
Barber, Karin. 2007. *The Anthropology of Texts, Persons and Publics: Oral and Written Culture in Africa and Beyond*. Cambridge: Cambridge University Press.
Barkow, Jerome, Leda Cosmides, and John Tooby, eds. 1995. *The Adapted Mind: Evolutionary Psychology and the Generation of Culture*. Oxford: Oxford University Press.
Basil, Priya. 2019. *Be My Guest: Reflections on Food, Community and the Meaning of Generosity*. Edinburgh: Cannongate Press.
Beck, Ulrich. 1992. *Risk Society: Towards a New Modernity*. London: Sage.
Bernard, H. Russell. 1976. "The Fisherman and His Wife." In *Oceans: Our Continuing Frontier*, ed. Henry William Menard and Jane L. Scheiber, 304–309. Del Mar, CA: Publisher's Inc.
Bittman, Mark. 2019. *Dinner for Everyone: 100 Iconic Dishes Made 3 Ways—Easy, Vegan, or Perfect for Company*. New York: Clarkson Potter.

Black, Rachel. 2021. *Cheffes de Cuisine: Women and Work in the Professional French Kitchen.* Urbana: University of Illinois Press.

Blanchette, Alex. 2020. *Porkopolis: American Animality, Standardized Life and the Factory Farm.* Durham, NC: Duke University Press.

Boholm, Asa. 2003. "The Cultural Nature of Risk: Can There Be an Anthropology of Uncertainty?" *Ethnos* 68(2): 159–78.

Bourdieu, Pierre. 1990. *The Logic of Practice*, trans. R. Nice. Stanford, CA: Stanford University Press.

Bryant, Rebecca, and Daniel Knight. 2019. *The Anthropology of the Future.* Cambridge: Cambridge University Press.

Brody, Jane. 1985. *Jane Brody's Good Food Book: Living the High-Carbohydrate Way.* New York: W.W. Norton.

Carrier, James. 2012. "Review of *Wall Street at War: The Secret Struggle for the Global Economy* by Alexandra Ouroussoff." *Journal of the Royal Anthropological Institute* 18(3): 703–4.

Carrier, James, and Daniel Miller, eds. 1998. *Virtualism.* Oxford: Berg.

Carsten, Janet, ed. 2007. *Ghosts of Memory: Essays on Remembrance and Relatedness.* Malden, MA: Blackwell Publishers.

Certeau, Michel de. 1984. *The Practice of Everyday Life Volume 1*, trans. Steven Rendall. Berkeley: University of California Press.

Certeau, Michel de, Luce Giard, and Pierre Mayol. 1998. *The Practice of Everyday Life Volume 2: Living and Cooking*, trans. Timothy J. Tomasick. Minneapolis: University of Minnesota Press.

Clark, Melissa. 2017. *Dinner: Changing the Game.* New York: Clarkson Potter.

Collier Jane. 1997. *From Duty to Desire: Remaking Families in a Spanish Village.* Princeton, NJ: Princeton University Press.

Comaroff, John. 2010. "The End of Anthropology, Again: On the Future of an In/Discipline." *American Anthropologist* 112(4): 524–38.

Comaroff, Jean, and John Comaroff. 1993. "Introduction." In *Modernity and Its Malcontents*, ed. Jean Comaroff and John Comaroff, xi–xxxvii. Chicago: University of Chicago Press.

Connerton, Paul. 1989. *How Societies Remember.* Cambridge: Cambridge University Press.

Counihan, Carole. 2004. *Around the Tuscan Table: Food, Family, and Gender in Twentieth-Century Florence.* New York: Routledge.

———. 2010. *A Tortilla Is Like Life: Food and Culture in the San Luis Valley.* Austin: University of Texas Press.

———. 2018. "Taste Activism in Urban Sardinia, Italy." In *Making Taste Public: Ethnographies of Food and the Senses*, ed. Carole Counihan and Susanne Hojlund, 155–68. London: Bloomsbury.

Crawford, Matthew. 2015. *The World beyond Your Head: On Becoming an Individual in an Age of Distraction.* New York: Farrar, Strauss & Giroux.

Daston, Lorraine. 2019. "SSRC Fellows Lecture: Lorraine Daston," speaking on Mechanical Rules before Machines: Rules and Paradigms, 12 February 2019. Retrieved 1 December 2020 from https://www.youtube.com/watch?v=6xErFnyjMAA&feature=share.

DeNicola, Alicia, and Clare Wilkinson-Weber. 2016. "Introduction: Taking Stock of Craft in Anthropology." In *Critical Craft: Technology, Globalization, Capitalism*, ed. Clare Wilkinson-Weber and Alicia DeNicola, 1–16. London: Bloomsbury.

Douglas Mary. 1974. "Deciphering a Meal." In *Food and Culture: A Reader*, ed. Carole Counihan and Penny van Esterik, 36–54. London: Routledge.

———. 1982. *In the Active Voice*. London: Routledge.

———. 1992. *Risk and Blame: Essays in Cultural Theory*. London: Routledge.

Doumanis, Nicholas. 1997. *Myth and Memory in the Mediterranean: Remembering Fascism's Empire*. London: Palgrave MacMillan.

Du Boulay, Juliet. 1974. *Portrait of a Greek Mountain Village*. Oxford: Clarendon.

Du Boulay, Juliet, and Rory Williams. 1987. "Amoral Familism and the Image of Limited Good: A Critique from a European Perspective." *Anthropological Quarterly* 60(1): 12–24.

Ellen, Roy, and Michael Fischer. 2013. "Introduction: On the Concept of Cultural Transmission." In *Understanding Cultural Transmission in Anthropology*, ed. R. Ellen, S. Lycett, and S. Johns, 1–54. New York: Berghahn.

Fernandez, James. 1966. "Unbelievably Subtle Words—Representation and Integration in the Sermons of an African Reformative Cult." *History of Religions* 6(1): 43–69.

Finn, John. 2011. "The Perfect Recipe: Taste and Tyranny, Cooks and Citizens." *Food, Culture and Society* 14(4): 503–24.

Firth, Rosemary. 1966. *Housekeeping among Malay Peasants*. 2nd edition. New York: Athlone.

Friedman, Jonathan. 1988. "No History Is an Island." *Critique of Anthropology* 8(3): 7–39.

Gabaccia, Donna. 1998. *We Are What We Eat: Ethnic Food and the Making of America*. Cambridge, MA: Harvard University Press.

Garot, Robert. 2015. "Gang-Banging as Edgework." *Dialectical Anthropology* 39: 151–63.

Garsten, Cristina, and Anna Hasselstrom. 2003. "Risky Business: Discourses of Risk and (Ir)responsibility in Globalizing Markets." *Ethnos* 68(2): 249–70.

Giard, Luce. 1998. "Part II: Doing-Cooking." In *The Practice of Everyday Life, Volume 2: Living and Cooking*, ed. Luce Giard, in association with Michel de Certeau and Pierre Mayol, trans. Timothy J. Tomasick, 149–248. Minneapolis: University of Minnesota Press.

Giddens, Anthony. 1999. "Risk and Responsibility." *The Modern Law Review* 62(1): 1–10.

Girardi, Robert. 2001. "Spaghetti." In *We Are What We Ate: 24 Memories of Food*, ed. Mark Winegardner, 93–104. New York: Harcourt Brace.

Golub, Alex, Daniel Rosenblatt, and John Kelly, eds. 2016. "Introduction: A Practice of Anthropology—The Work of Marshall Sahlins, So Far." In *A Practice of Anthropology: The Thought and Influence of Marshall Sahlins*. Montreal: McGill-Queens University Press.

Gowlland, Geoffrey. 2017. "Thinking through Materials: Embodied Problem Solving and the Values of Work in Taiwanese Ceramics." In *Craftwork as Problem Solving: Ethnographic Studies of Design and Making*, ed. Trevor Marchand, 183–96. New York: Routledge.

Gvion, Liora. 2012. *Beyond Hummus and Falafel: Social and Political Aspects of Palestinian Food in Israel*. Berkeley: University of California Press.

Halkias, Alexandra. 2004. *Empty Cradle of Democracy: Sex, Abortion and Nationalism in Modern Greece*. Durham, NC: Duke University Press.

Hallam, Elizabeth, and Tim Ingold. 2007. "Introduction." *Creativity and Cultural Improvisation*, ed. Elizabeth Hallam and Tim Ingold, 1–24. Oxford, UK: Berg.

Hamilakis, Yannis. 2008. "Decolonizing Greek Archaeology: Indigenous Archaeologies, Modernist Archaeology and the Post-Colonial Critique." Benaki Museum, 3rd Supplement. *A Singular Antiquity*, ed. Dimitris Damaskos and Dimitris Plantzos, 273–84. https://doi.org/10.12681/benaki.18044.

———. 2014. *Archaeology and the Senses: Human Experience, Memory, Affect*. Cambridge: Cambridge University Press.

Harper, Paul W.H. 2013. *Doing and Talking: The Value of Video Interviewing for Researching and Theorizing Craft*. Ph.D. dissertation. London: London Metropolitan University.

Hauck-Lawson, Annie. 1998. "When Food Is the Voice: A Case Study of a Polish-American Woman." *Journal for the Study of Food and Society* 2(1): 21–28.

Hayden, Delores. 1982. *The Grand Domestic Revolution: A History of Feminist Designs for American Homes, Neighborhoods, and Cities*. Cambridge, MA: MIT Press.

Heinrich, H-A, and V. Weyland. 2016. "Communicative and Cultural Memory as a Micro-mesomacro Relation." *International Journal of Media and Cultural Politics* 12(1): 27–41.

Heldke, Lisa. 1992. "Foodmaking as Thoughtful Practice." In *Cooking Eating, Thinking: Transformative Philosophies of Food*, ed. Deane Curtin and Lisa Heldke, 203–29. Bloomington, IN: Indiana University Press.

Herzfeld, Michael. 1985. *The Poetics of Manhood*. Princeton, NJ: Princeton University Press.

———. 1992. *The Social Production of Indifference: Exploring the Symbolic Roots of Western Bureaucracy*. Oxford: Berg.

———. 1997. *Cultural Intimacy: Social Poetics in the Nation-State*. London: Routledge.

Hirsch, Eric, and Charles Stewart. 2005. "Introduction: Ethnographies of Historicity." *History and Anthropology* 16(3): 261–74.

Hojer, Lars, and Andreas Bandak. 2015. "Introduction: The Power of Example." Special Issue *The Power of Example: Anthropological Explorations in Persuasion, Evocation and Imitation. JRAI* 21(S1): 1–17.

Holtzman, Jon. 2009. *Uncertain Tastes: Memory, Ambivalence and the Politics of Eating in Samburu, Northern Kenya*. Berkeley: University of California Press.

Howard, Penny. 2018. "The Anthropology of Human-Environment Relations: Materialism with and without Marxism." *Focaal—Journal of Global and Historical Anthropology* 82: 64–79.

Howes, David. 2003. *Sensual Relations: Engaging the Senses in Culture and Social Theory*. Ann Arbor: University of Michigan Press.

Ingold, Tim. 2000. *The Perception of the Environment: Essays in Livelihood, Dwelling and Skill*. London: Routledge.

———. 2001. "From the Transmission of Representations to the Education of Attention." In *The Debated Mind: Evolutionary Psychology Versus Ethnography*, ed. Harvey Whitehouse, 113–153. New York: Berg.

———. 2011. *Being Alive: Essays on Movement, Knowledge and Description*. London: Routledge.

———. 2013. *Making: Anthropology, Archaeology, Art and Architecture*. London: Routledge.

Janeja, Manpreet. 2010. *Transactions in Taste: The Collaborative Lives of Everyday Bengali Food*. London: Routledge.

Jones, Graham. 2011. *Trade of the Tricks: Inside the Magician's Craft*. Berkeley: University of California Press.

Kalafatas, Michael. 2003. *The Bellstone: The Greek Sponge Divers of the Aegean: One American's Journey Home*. Waltham, MA: Brandeis University Press.

Kalantzis, Kostis. 2020. "Memory in Athens: Acquiescent Spreaders, Occidentalism and Peripatetic Memory in Athens, Greece." Maxwell Museum of Anthropology, *Covid-19 Exhibition*. Retrieved 1 December 2020 from https://www.covid19exhibition.org/sickness-chapter-4.

Kapferer, Bruce. 2015. "Introduction." In *In the Event: Toward an Anthropology of Generic Moments*, ed. L. Meinhart and B. Kapferer, 1–28. New York: Berghahn.

Keller, Charles, and Janet Keller. 1999. "Imagery in Cultural Tradition and Innovation." *Mind, Culture and Activity* 6: 3–32.

Knight, Daniel. 2012. "Cultural Proximity: Crisis, Time and Social Memory in Central Greece." *History and Anthropology* 23(3): 349–74.

———. 2015. *History, Time and Economic Crisis in Central Greece*. New York: Palgrave MacMillan.

Lahne, Jacob, and Christy Spackman. 2018. "Introduction to *Accounting for Taste*." *The Senses and Society* 13(1): 1–5.

Latour, Bruno. 1993. *We Have Never Been Modern*, trans. Catherine Porter. Cambridge, MA: Harvard University Press.

Lears, T. Jackson. 2019. "Art for Life's Sake: Craft and the Quest for Wholeness in American Culture." *Journal of Modern Craft* 12(2): 161–72.

Lee, Mandy. 2019. *The Art of Escapism Cooking: A Survival Story, with Intensely Good Flavors*. New York: William Morrow.

Lewis, Tania. 2020. *Digital Food: From Paddock to Platform*. London: Bloomsbury.

Li, Victor. 2001. "Marshall Sahlins and the Apotheosis of Culture." *The New Centennial Review* 1(3): 201–87.

L'Orange Furst, Elisabeth. 1997. "Cooking and Femininity." *Women's Studies International Forum* 20 (3): 441–49.

Malaby, Thomas. 2003. *Gambling Life: Dealing in Contingency in a Greek City*. Champaign: University of Illinois Press.

Mann, Anna. 2015. *Tasting in Mundane Practices: Ethnographic Interventions in Social Science Theory*. Amsterdam: University of Amsterdam, Digital Academic Repository.

Metcalf, Bruce. 2007. "Replacing the Myth of Modernism." In *Neocraft: Modernity and the Arts*, ed. Sandra Alfoldy, 4–32. Nova Scotia: Nova Scotia College of Art and Design Press.

Miller, Daniel. 2010. *Stuff*. London: Polity.

Mintz, Sidney. 1997. *Tasting Food, Tasting Freedom*. Boston: Beacon.

Mintz, Sidney, and Richard Price. 1992. *The Birth of African-American Culture: An Anthropological Approach*. Boston: Beacon Press.

Morozov, Evgeny. 2013. *To Save Everything, Click Here: The Folly of Technological Solutionism*. New York: Public Affairs Press.

Morris, Kathleen. 2016. "You Are Not a Lemming: The Imagined Resistance of Craft Citizenship." *Journal of Modern Craft* 9(1): 5–14.

Newmahr, Staci. 2011. "Chaos, Order, and Collaboration: Toward a Feminist Conceptualization of Edgework." *Journal of Contemporary Ethnography* 40(6): 682–712.

Obyesekere, Gananath. 1992. *The Apotheosis of Captain Cook*. Princeton, NJ: Princeton University Press.

Orlando, Giovanni. 2018. "From the Risk Society to Risk Practice: Organic Food, Embodiment and Modernity in Sicily." *Food, Culture and Society* 21(2): 144–63.

Palmer, Catherine. 2002. "'Shit Happens': The Selling of Risk in Extreme Sport." *Australian Journal of Anthropology* 13(3): 323–36.

Palmié, Stephan. 2013. *The Cooking of History: How Not to Study Afro-Cuban Religion*. Chicago: University of Chicago Press.

Palmié, Stephan, and Charles Stewart. 2016. "Introduction: For an Anthropology of History." *Hau: Journal of Ethnographic Theory* 6(1): 207–36

Panourgia, Neni. 2009. *Dangerous Citizens: The Greek Left and the Terror of the State*. New York: Fordham University Press.

Papacharalampous, Nafsika. 2019. *The Metamorphosis of Greek Cuisine: Sociability, Precarity and Foodways of Crisis in Middle Class Athens*. Ph.D. dissertation. London: SOAS University of London.

Parveen, Razia. 2017. *Recipes and Songs: An Analysis of Cultural Practices from South Asia*. London: Palgrave MacMillan.

Paxson, Heather. 2004. *Making Modern Mothers: Ethics and Family Planning in Urban Greece*. Berkeley: University of California Press.

———. 2011. "The 'Art' and 'Science' of Handcrafting Cheese in the United States." *Endeavour* 35(2–3): 116–24.

———. 2013. *The Life of Cheese: Crafting Food and Value in the United States*. Berkeley: University of California Press.

Pipyrou, Stavroula. 2016. *The Grecanici of Southern Italy: Government, Violence and Minority Politics*. Philadelphia: University of Pennsylvania Press.

Pollan, Michael. 2020. "The Sickness in Our Food Supply." *The New York Review of Books*, 11 June. Retrieved 1 December 2020 from https://www.nybooks.com/articles/2020/06/11/covid-19-sickness-food-supply/.

Press, Mike. 2007. "Handmade Futures: The Emerging Role of Craft in Our Digital Culture. In *Neocraft: Modernity and the Arts*, ed. Sandra Alfoldy, 249–66. Halifax: Nova Scotia College of Art and Design Press.

Portisch, Anna. 2010. "The Craft of Skillful Learning: Kazakh Craftswomen of Western Mongolia." *Making Knowledge: Special Issue of the Journal of the Royal Anthropological Institute* 16(S1): 62–79.

Pye, David. 1968. *The Nature and Art of Workmanship*. Cambridge: Cambridge University Press.

———. 1969. *The Nature of Design*. London: Studio Vista.

Reyna, Stephen. 1997. "Theory in Anthropology in the Nineties." *Cultural Dynamics* 9: 209–31.

Richards, Audrey. 1939. *Land, Labour and Diet in Northern Rhodesia: An Economic Study among the Bemba Tribe*. London: Oxford University Press.

Robbins Joel. 2016. "How Long is the Longue Duree? Structure, Duration and the Cultural Analysis of Cultural Change." In *A Practice of Anthropology: The Thought and Influence of Marshall Sahlins,* ed. Alex Golub, Daniel Rosenblatt and John Kelly, 40–62. Montreal: McGill-Queens University Press.

Roden, Claudia. 1986. *A New Book of Middle Eastern Food*. New York: Penguin.

Roosth, Sophia. 2013. "Of Foams and Formalisms: Scientific Expertise and Craft Practice in Molecular Gastronomy." *American Anthropologist* 115(1): 4–16.

Sahlins, Marshall. 1985. *Islands of History*. Chicago: University of Chicago Press.

———. 2004 *Apologies to Thucydides: Understanding History as Culture and Vice Versa*. Chicago: University of Chicago Press.

———. 2005a. *Culture in Practice: Selected Essays*. New York: Zone Books.

———. 2005b. "Structural Work: How Microhistories become Macrohistories and Vice Versa." *Anthropological Theory* 5(1): 5–30.

Salamone, S. D., and J. B. Stanton. 1986. "Introducing the Nikokyra: Ideality and Reality in Social Process." In *Gender and Power in Rural Greece*, ed. Jill Dubisch, 97–120. Princeton, NJ: Princeton University Press.

Schneider, Sally. 2006. *The Improvisational Cook*. New York: Harper-Collins.

Schweitzer-Gil, Andrea. 2020. "Sharing Food while Being Apart: Synaesthesia in the Time of Covid-19." *Synesthesia: Sixth Sense Abcderium*. Retrieved 1 December 2020 from https://sixthsensereader.org/.

Scott, James. 1998. *Seeing Like a State: How Certain Schemes to Improve the Human Condition Have Failed*. New Haven, CT: Yale University Press.

Sennett, Richard. 2008. *The Craftsman*. New Haven, CT: Yale University Press.

Seremetakis, C. Nadia. 1994. "The Memory of the Senses: Parts 1&2." In *The Senses Still: Perception and Memory as Material Culture in Modernity*, ed. C. N. Seremetakis, 1–43. Boulder, CO: Westview Press.

———. 2019. *Sensing the Everyday: Dialogues from Austerity Greece*. Abingdon: Taylor & Francis.

Sewell, William. 2005. *Logics of History: Social Theory and Social Transformation*. Chicago: University of Chicago Press.

Shields-Argeles, Christy. 2018. "Tasting Comte Cheese, Returning to the Whole: The *Jury Terroir* as Ritual Practice." In *Making Taste Public: Ethnographies of Food and the Senses*, ed. Carole Counihan and Susanne Hojlund, 83–96. London: Bloomsbury.

Short, Frances. 2006. *Kitchen Secrets: The Meaning of Cooking in Everyday Life*. Oxford: Berg.

Shove, Elizabeth, Mika Pantzar, and Matt Watson. 2012. *The Dynamics of Social Practice: Everyday Life and How it Changes*. London: Sage.

Sifton, Sam. 2016. "Go for Gold: Oven-Roasted Hash Browns Make a Blank Canvas for Breakfast, Lunch or Dinner." *New York Times Magazine*, 7 August, 26–27.

Sperber, Dan. 1996. *Explaining Culture: A Naturalistic Approach*. London: Blackwell.

Steinmetz, George. 2008. "Logics of History as a Framework for an Integrated Social Science." *Social Science History* 32(4): 535–53.

Stewart, Charles. 2012. *Dreaming and Historical Consciousness in Island Greece*. Cambridge, MA: Harvard University Press.

———. 2016. "Historicity and Anthropology." *Annual Review of Anthropology* 45: 79–94.

———. 2017. "Uncanny History: Temporal Topology in the Post-Ottoman World." *Social Analysis* 61(1): 129–42.

Suchman, Lucy. 2007. *Human-Machine Reconfigurations: Plans and Situated Action*. Cambridge: Cambridge University Press.

Sutton, David. 1994. "Tradition & Modernity: Kalymnian Constructions of Identity & Otherness." *Journal of Modern Greek Studies* 12: 239–60.

———. 1998. *Memories Cast in Stone: The Relevance of the Past in Everyday Life*. Oxford: Berg.

———. 2001. *Remembrance of Repasts: An Anthropology of Food and Memory*. Oxford: Berg.

———. 2003. "The Foreign Finger: Conspiracy Theory as Holistic Thinking in Greece." In *The Usable Past: Greek Metahistories*, ed. Keith Brown and Yiannis Hamilakis. 191–208. Lanham, MD: Rowman & Littlefield.

———. 2004. "Ritual, Continuity and Change." *History and Anthropology* 15 (2): 91–105.

———. 2006. "Cooking Skills, the Senses and Memory: The Fate of Practical Knowledge." In *Sensible Objects: Colonialism, Museums and Material Culture*, ed. Chris Gosden, Elizabeth Edwards, and Ruth Phillips, 87–118. Oxford: Berg.

————. 2008. "Tradition and Modernity Revisited: Existential Memory Work on a Greek Island." *History and Memory* 20: 84–105.

————. 2011. "The Sensory Experience of Food: Memory as a Sense." Invited Roundtable with Carolyn Korsmeyer. *Food, Culture and Society* 14(4): 468–75.

————. 2014. *Secrets from the Greek Kitchen: Cooking, Skill and Everyday Life on a Greek Island*. Berkeley: University of California Press.

————. 2016a. "The Anthropology of Cooking." *Handbook of Food and Anthropology*, ed. Jakob Klein and James Watson, 349–69. London: Bloomsbury.

————. 2016b. "'Let Them Eat Stuffed Peppers': An Argument of Images on the Role of Food in Understanding Neoliberal Austerity in Greece." *Gastronomica: The Journal of Critical Food Studies* 16(4): 8–17.

————. 2017. "Review Essay: How to Cook Herring, and Other Puzzles of Modern, Distracted Life." *Social Anthropology* 25(4): 546–50.

————. 2018. "Cooking in Theory: Risky Events in the Structure of the Conjuncture." *Anthropological Theory* 18(1): 81–105.

————. 2021. "Revivifying Commensality: Eating, Politics and the Sensory Production of the Social." In *Itineraries and Sanctuaries in Contemporary Food Studies*, ed. Virginia Nazarea and Terese Gagnon, 133–160. Tucson: University of Arizona Press.

Sutton, David, and Peter Wogan. 2009. *Hollywood Blockbusters: The Anthropology of Popular Movies*. Oxford: Berg.

Swinbank, Vicki. 2002. "The Sexual Politics of Cooking: A Feminist Analysis of Culinary Hierarchy in Western Culture." *Journal of Historical Sociology* 15(4): 464–94.

Symons, Michael. 2003. *A History of Cooks and Cooking*. Urbana: University of Illinois Press.

Terrio, Susan. 2000. *Crafting the Culture and History of French Chocolate*. Berkeley: University of California Press.

Theodossopoulos, Dimitrios. 2014. "On De-Pathologizing Resistance." *History and Anthropology* 25(4): 415–30.

Toren, Christina. 2001. *Mind, Materiality and History: Explorations in Fijian Ethnography*. London: Routledge.

Tracy, Sarah. 2018. "Delicious Molecules: Big Food Science, the Chemosenses, and Umami." *The Senses and Society* 13(1): 89–107.

Trubek, Amy. 2017. *Making Modern Meals: How Americans Cook Today*. Berkeley: University of California Press.

Trubek, Amy, Maria Carabello, Caitlin Morgan, and Jacob Lahne. 2017. "Empowered to Cook: The Crucial Role of 'Food Agency' in Making Meals." *Appetite* 116: 297–305.

Urban, Greg. 2001. *Metaculture: How Culture Moves through the World*. Minneapolis: University of Minnesota Press.

————. 2010. "A Method for Measuring the Motion of Culture." *American Anthropologist* 112(1): 122–39.

Van Daele, Wim. 2015. "Food's Entanglements with Life: How Is It Good to Work with?" Conference Call for Papers, University of Oslo. Overheating seminar.

Van Dooremalen, Thijs. 2017. "The Pros and Cons of Researching Events Ethnographically." *Ethnography* 18(3): 415–24.

Vournelis, Leonidas. 2013. "Paying the Check, Eating the Money: Food-Based Challenges to Neoliberalism in Greece." *Food, Culture and Society* 16(3): 354–59.

Wagner-Pacifici, Robin. 2017. *What Is an Event?* Chicago: University of Chicago Press.

Warde, Alan. 2016. *The Practice of Eating*. London: Polity.

Weiner, Margaret. 2015. "Island Cooking." Book Symposium, Comment on Palmié. *Hau* 5(1): 535–40.

Weiss, Brad. 1996. *The Making and Unmaking of the Haya Lived World: Consumption, Commoditization and Everyday Practice.* Durham, NC: Duke University Press.

West, Harry. 2020. "Crafting Innovation: Continuity and Change in the 'Living Traditions' of Contemporary Artisan Cheesemakers." *Food and Foodways* 28(2): 91–116.

Wilk, Richard. 2006. *Home Cooking in the Global Village: Caribbean Food from Buccaneers to Ecotourists.* Oxford: Berg.

Wilson, Bee. 2012. *Consider the Fork: A History of How We Cook What We Eat.* New York: Basic Books.

Yalouri, Eleana. 2014. "Possessing Antiquity: Reconnecting to the Past in the Greek Present." In *Reimagining the Past: Antiquity and Modern Greek Culture*, ed. Dimitris Tziovas, 165–85. Oxford: Oxford University Press.

———. 2018. "The Return of the Unreal." *Field: A Journal of Socially Engaged Art Criticism* 11(fall). http://field-journal.com/issue-11/the-return-of-the-unreal.

Yarbrough, Steve. 2001. "Grandma's Table." In *We Are What We Ate: 24 Memories of Food*, ed. Mark Winegardner, 205–20. New York: Harcourt Brace.

Yong, Ed. 2016. *I Contain Multitudes: The Microbes within Us and a Grander View of Life.* New York: Harper Collins.

Zeitlyn, David. 2015. "Looking Forward, Looking Back." *History and Anthropology* 26(4): 381–407.

Zinn, Jens. 2019. *Understanding Risk Taking.* Critical Studies in Risk and Uncertainty. New York: Palgrave.

INDEX

༄

Printed in the USA
CPSIA information can be obtained
at www.ICGtesting.com
JSHW050929180923
48625JS00008B/50

9 781805 391135